D0949023

FOR Wildcats Fans ONLY!

Wonderful Stories Celebrating the Incredible Fans of the Kansas State Wildcats

By Kent Pulliam and Rich Wolfe

Foreword by Wildcat Greats, Players, Coaches, and Fans

www.ascendbooks.com

10 9 8 7 6 5 4 3 2 1

Printed in the United States of America

ISBN-13: 978-0-9841130-0-2
ISBN-10: 0-9841130-0-2

Library of Congress Cataloging-in-Publications Data Available Upon Request

Editor: Lee Stuart
Design: Randy Lackey, The Covington Group

This book is not an official publication of, nor is it endorsed by, Kansas State University.

www.ascendbooks.com

FOR Wildcats Fans ONLY!

**Wonderful Stories Celebrating the Incredible
Fans of the Kansas State Wildcats**

The fans say it all – K-State loves those Wildcats.

Photo courtesy of Anson "Buster" Renshaw

Photo courtesy of Christopher Hanewinckel

Special Thanks To:

Table of Contents

Foreword
A Collection of Favorite Memories from Kansas State Fans

I have had the pleasure and the good fortune to be able to travel throughout the entire state for almost six decades, meeting people in all walks of life. You find K-State people to be very, very friendly; very, very professional; and very easy to get acquainted with, and a joy to be around.

Ernie Barrett – "Mr. K-State"

The Kansas State University fan has been one of great perseverance. They have bounced off the canvas time and time again, having gone through the suffering and lived through it and fought through it and come out in the end.

That's the nature of the Kansas State fan.

Whether it happens to be in football or happens to be in basketball, there is a perseverance that says we are going to get through this and will fight our way back. They are fans – not that they are a football fan or a basketball fan, they are a Kansas State fan.

They have a unique passion for their football and athletic programs.

I have always found them very passionate, very prideful, normally very humble, very caring and supportive. They have a real sense of caring about not just the wins and losses but about the young people who participate and the intrinsic value promoted by our program to help them develop. They appreciate that.

Bill Snyder – Legendary Coach

They are a wonderful lot, these K-State fans. You want them as family friends. You want them as business partners. They are loyal. They are passionate, and they are resilient.

Mitch Holthus – Former Voice of the Wildcats

It takes a special person to be a Kansas State fan. You'd better be tough. You'd better be resilient. If you are a fighter, you'd better be able to take a punch.

Kevin Kietzman – K-State alumnus and Radio Show Host

(Living in Lawrence), every once in a while I get waved at with one finger, but I just assume they are busy and didn't have time to put up the other four.

Lora Gilliland-Schneider – K-State alumna living in Lawrence

I bet you I hold the record for the most speeding tickets going from Wichita to K-State. I got four of them one night!

George Schultz – K-State Fan in a Hurry

I went to the bathroom at halftime and sold my soul to the devil if we could just win that game (the 2003 Big 12 Championship).

Leon Roberts – A K-State Fan Who No Longer Has a Soul

I think our alumni group here probably drinks a little more beer when we lose.

Jill Vinduska – Leader of K-State Fans in Florida

CHAPTER 1

Purple Pride

"Every man a Wildcat."

"We Gonna Win!"

"Eat-em–up, Eat-em-up, K-S-U!"

"Purple Pride."

Kansas State fans are passionate, wearing their purple proudly, posting a Powercat decal in the center of their license plates, and cheering for the Wildcat athletic teams – for better and worse.

And there has been plenty of both.

Long-time fans suffered through years of the worst college football in history and cheered the basketball team's success.

A new generation of fans has cheered unprecedented success on the football field with conference championships and an 11-year stretch of bowl games.

Women's sports, which have relied heavily on the recruitment of home-grown athletes from small towns across the state, have won conference championships and post-season tournaments.

Kansas State fans are not only from every corner of Kansas, but they also live throughout the country. There are Spirit Clubs or Catbacker clubs in 37 states and the District of Columbia. They wear their purple to game-watching parties as proudly as anyone sitting in the stands at Bill Snyder Family Stadium or Bramlage Coliseum.

They devour every morsel of news from every possible resource: newspapers, radio, television, and the internet. Any perceived slight is met with outrage normally reserved for a jilted lover.

They have been instrumental in the success of their teams from Ahearn Field House – the Old Barn – where they sat so close to the sidelines that they could harass opponents with dead chickens or pop guns, to the raucous crowd that saw the 30-game losing streak to Nebraska end on a cold November night in 1998 at KSU Stadium.

They have been euphoric after the men's basketball team won 84-75 over Kansas in 2008 – the first K-State victory over the Jayhawks at Bramlage Coliseum – and beside themselves after a 35-7 rout of Oklahoma in the Big 12 Football Championship game in Arrowhead Stadium in 2003.

And they have been distraught when the chance to play for the BCS football championship slipped through their fingers in 1998 when they fell 36-33 in two overtimes to Texas A&M after cruising through the conference season with an average winning margin of 29 points per game.

They span the years from Jack Gardner to Frank Martin, Vince Gibson to Bill Snyder to ... Bill Snyder again.

More importantly, they have established a community of friends where purple is the only entry fee. They are the type of people you want to have as friends, with a sense of humor, a sense of humility, and the kind of hard-working ethic that is true Kansas.

The sense of humor is best exemplified by a story about one of former football Coach Vince Gibson's early forays out into the state to stir up Purple Pride. He was accompanied by Ernie Barrett, who reminded him that above all he should recognize Forrest Brookover, one of the donors in the crowd of this gathering in Scott City, Kansas.

> In 1972, Oklahoma beat K-State, 52-0.
>
> K-State was lucky to score 0.

Gibson got wound up, as he was prone to do. And his speech, delivered with the zeal of a revival preacher, went on and on. Barrett was fearful that the football coach had forgotten to mention Brookover.

But Gibson ended the speech with a thanks for all who had made the gathering possible and a special thank you to "Trees Overbrook."

The crowd erupted in laughter, including Brookover, who henceforth was known by the nickname "Trees."

While basketball was Kansas State's athletic currency through much of the last half-century, football became its king as K-State fans embraced the simple philosophy of incremental improvement preached by Coach Bill Snyder.

Work hard to be better today than you were yesterday. Work even harder to be better tomorrow than you were today. It fits the small-town ethic of work: you do things for yourself rather than wait for someone to do them for you.

And K-State fans have this wonderful chip on their shoulder that allows them to pick themselves up off the canvas after a knockdown and continue on with perseverance.

Through it all, the band has played:

"Fight you K-State Wildcats. For Alma Mater fight-fight-fight."

"Glory into combat for the purple and the white. Faithful to our colors, we shall ever be, fighting ever fighting for a Wildcat Victory!"

And since 1969, the "Wabash Cannonball" has been a second fight song. Because of a fire at the school's music department, only the sheet music in the band director's brief case – which happened to be the "Wabash Cannonball" – survived. That song has since been adopted as a rollicking musical celebration at K-State games.

❋ ❋ ❋

ERNIE BARRETT
Manhattan, Kansas

Barrett, an All-America basketball player who led K-State to the Final Four in 1951, has stumped for the school for the better part of 60 years – as athletic director from 1969-75 and as an ambassador for more years that anyone can count. He is known as "Mr. Kansas State" and has met virtually every K-State fan of the past 50 years. He has enjoyed every one of them.

I have had the pleasure and the good fortune to be able to travel throughout the entire state for almost six decades, meeting people in all walks of life. You find K-State people to be very, very friendly; very, very professional; and very easy to get acquainted with, and a joy to be around.

You can go out to western Kansas and walk into a K-Stater's office. You don't need an appointment. You don't need to call in advance or anything else to let them know you are going to be there. They are just happy to see you. There are not a lot of people who have traveled throughout western Kansas. I have always called western Kansas the garden spot of America because the people out there are just so friendly and happy to see you. It's rewarding to be able to see them and be able to talk to them.

We have fans all over the country, and I have attended a bunch of watch parties throughout the country. They are fun to go to. People are happy to see someone from K-State and to visit with them. When you would ask them how often they got back to K-State, the majority of them said "Never."

We had a lot of lean years when we didn't win in football. Then Coach Snyder came on board and proved everybody wrong. I had always thought we could win in football if we had the right leadership. Snyder presented that.

Everybody loves a winner. What Snyder did was come in here and prove to our fans and our alumni that we could win here in football.

ROBERT LIPSON
Manhattan, Kansas

If Barrett is the quintessential K-Stater, Robert is perhaps the quintessential K-State fan. He has a string of 37 consecutive years in which he has attended every conference football game the Wildcats have played. While not a large donor to the school, Lipson is known throughout the conference.

It's by random coincidence that I came out here. I had never been farther west than the New Jersey turnpike my entire life. When I first looked at the catalogue for colleges at the Farmingdale College Library, I was looking at Kansas State. They had everything I was looking for to study.

As I was reading the catalogue, what I knew about it was that Gale Sayers had played there. Wilt Chamberlain had played there. They had 12 men on the field against Pennsylvania State in the Orange Bowl. So I thought, "What do you know? I am going to be a Jayhawk."

Nobody back home knew there were two schools, so it came as a complete surprise to me that I was a Wildcat.

I came to Kansas State because at the time it had more of what I wanted at the undergraduate level. I was interested in certain things in biology. Kansas State had them at the undergraduate level. They were unique in that they had some courses where the undergraduate and the graduate student could attend the exact same class and get their respective credits.

❝ Nobody back home knew there were two schools (in Kansas), so it came as a complete surprise to me that I was a Wildcat. ❞

I always liked sports and wanted to go to the games. I don't know how to explain to people how I became a fan except that when I saw how the students and fans reacted to how the team was trailing in a game, I got swept off my feet by them. If the basketball team was losing their lead or was behind during a game, the students, especially, would get up and yell and cheer. They were proactive instead of reactive. You didn't see that anywhere else.

I wanted to see what the rest of the conference looked like, so I went to Missouri and Kansas and Nebraska in the winter of 1973. I saw those places for the very first time. I have kept going ever since.

I started something that actually continues to this day – going to road games in conference play with the football team. I have all the tickets in the exact order in a safe deposit box. I have not missed a conference game in road play. I can't imagine missing a game. That would be like dying. I don't know how I could possibly miss one right now. As more time goes on, the worse it would be. That would be 37 years of my life all wasted. I don't know how I could cope with that.

I worry about it all the time – that something catastrophic would happen and I can't get to a road game. I take off as early as Wednesday to buy myself time for a road game at Texas or Texas A&M or Texas Tech or Colorado.

Imagine what a catastrophe it would be for the world of college athletics if I were to miss a road game in conference play. It's unthinkable!

People see me at tailgates at home games; quite a few know who I am. At the road games, I am getting to know quite a few. Among the old Big 8 people there are some class acts that I got to know from all over the conference. I tell these class acts to come to Manhattan when you return the game at our stadium.

The Buffaloes at Boulder is always the best road game in the conference. Just look toward the west on a clear day and you will see why. It's spectacular.

BILL SNYDER
Head football coach

Snyder became head football coach in 1989 and supervised the "Miracle in Manhattan," reviving a left-for-dead football program. From the beginning, he knew that the support of Kansas State fans was going to be one of the building blocks to the football team's success, and he tapped into that from the 13,000 who supported the Wildcats when he arrived to the 50,000-plus who filled a stadium that was expanded twice during the 1990s. After retiring in 2005, he is back for a second tenure as Kansas State football coach.

The Kansas State University fan has been one of great perseverance. They have bounced off the canvas time and time again, having gone through the suffering and lived through it and fought through it and come out in the end.

That's the nature of the Kansas State fan.

Whether it happens to be in football or happens to be in basketball, there is a perseverance that says we are going to get through this and will fight our way back. They are fans – not that they are a football fan or a basketball fan, they are a *Kansas State fan*.

They have a unique passion for their football and athletic programs. For them to have that tremendous passion and that great sense of their pride through those really difficult years really said an awful lot about those 13,000 who were there (in 1989).

I have always found them very passionate, very prideful, normally very humble, very caring and supportive. They have a real sense of caring about not just the wins and losses but about the young people who participate and the intrinsic value promoted by our program to help them develop. They appreciate that.

When I was retired, I got around and met a lot more people who I normally didn't get to spend time with. It re-emphasized what I thought I knew – that they were very gracious and caring people. That really came to light during the three years I was not coaching.

In 1989 when we were first getting started, I felt that passion. When we got here, the average attendance at the games prior to the year I came had been 13,000. You might remember there was an NCAA rule in place that indicated you have to have an average attendance of 19,000 to be a Division I football program.

The Board of Regents had discussions about what would have happened if the NCAA enforced its policy. There were discussions about dropping football at Kansas State or reducing it to what we called 1-AA. Either of those consequences would have had a dramatic impact on this school and it would not be what it is today. It would have been devastating.

That 13,000 over a period of years became 19,000, then 35,000, then 45,000, and eventually 50,000. My approach that first year was that it wasn't going to be like a field of dreams. It wasn't going to be you build it and they will come. I emphasized to our fans it was extremely important that they come. They would be the foundation for building the program. I always referred to those 13,000 who were there during those very difficult times as the real Kansas State faithful and the foundation for Kansas State football over a period of years.

When they were in the stands, the players would gain a great deal of motivation from that. Over a period of time their performance level would improve because the performance level of our fans had improved because of the attendance. They seemingly appreciated that approach or at least respected it enough to make it happen that way. The rest is kind of history.

But 1993 is when it really was put into perspective for me. A gentleman came from Goodland, Kansas, drove to Manhattan to tell me that going to the Copper Bowl was the greatest event in his life. I think about that all the time. I know he didn't deem the game of football to be more significant than his family or his career or all the things that had happened in his life.

But it was his way of stating the passion he had for Kansas State football. That really put it in perspective for me. I accepted his feelings as being representative of a large base of Kansas State people. It really put it in perspective for me how much all this means to the Kansas State fans, who had suffered so very much.

JOHN CURRIE
Kansas State athletic director

Currie has been on the job only since June 8, 2009, but he was an associate athletic director at Tennessee when the Volunteers played Kansas State in the 2001 Cotton Bowl. That snowy, cold morning in Dallas convinced him there was something special about the K-State faithful.

It was awful cold that morning, and I have to be honest, there were a few people in our travel party at Tennessee who did not make it out of the hotel that day. My wife, Mary Lawrence, was seven months pregnant with our first child. But we pulled on a few extra layers of clothing and went over to that historic fairgrounds and historic stadium. We walked in there and the first thing we saw were 55,000 – or whatever it was – K-State fans. They were oblivious to the cold, and they were going crazy and singing and cheering for their team. It was just unbelievable, really impressive. That really set the stage for me to look into it when this job came open.

The more I dug into it and did research on K-State and talked to people around the country, the more excited I was about Kansas State. As you get here, you see it is the quintessential American university. It's a university town, beautiful surroundings, beautiful campus and great people with a real attitude of getting things done all the way across campus, not just in athletics.

My first day in the office I worked a long day and then went to Great Bend for a Catbacker event. There were 200 people in Great Bend. The next night we went to Hutchinson and another 200 people. Two days later we were in Wichita and had 500-600 there.

One of the great things is that I have met a lot of people who didn't go to Kansas State but were very passionate about Kansas State because they identify with the work ethic of the people of Kansas. And of course Kansas State University is in every county of the state with its extension service, and it really is the university of the people of Kansas.

There is a similarity with Tennessee and Kansas State in that both have a passionate fan base. In some years Tennessee might have been able to do a few more things because it has a little larger budget. Kansas State has a history of getting it done with fewer resources. That's another thing that is really special about this place.

MITCH HOLTHUS
Radio Voice of the Wildcats from 1983-1996

Holthus is a 1979 graduate of Kansas State and was the radio voice of the Wildcats from 1983-96, observing first-hand some of the glory seasons of basketball and the start of the football ascendance in the 1990s.

Kansas State is truly a unique place. I know now it is even more unique as I have become somewhat removed and on the outside looking in, and being exposed to other schools around the country.

Kansas State, from its beginning, has always had to fight for its place. In the 1860s, the Kansas legislature – both the Senate and the House – passed a measure to put the state university in Manhattan because Manhattan already had a school, Bluemont College.

It got vetoed by the governor, who was from Lawrence. They couldn't override the veto, so bada-bing, the University of Kansas was formed. From that time, K-State has always had to fight and scrap and claw and battle finances and politics and kind of work uphill. K-State fans are a parallel to the school.

They are battle-hardened because they live every day like that. The wind is rarely blowing at their back. I don't say that to whine for them. It's just the fight they had. They are always fighting for their spot.

They are loyal, dedicated and resilient. K-State's good fans are some of the most loyal, resilient fans I have ever seen. That's why it was so exhilarating in the 1990s to see people rewarded for their resiliency. They were one snap from playing in the (football) National Championship game (in 1998). They went to 11 straight bowl games. It was heart-warming to see them get rewarded.

They became the land-grant school that was now a big player. But they were still one step in the shadow.

K-Staters, if they are born into it and raised with it, learn they have to fight for their place all the time. They are always on the alert, kind of edgy. If they are thin-skinned, it is because they have had to be thin-skinned all their life because nothing has ever come easy to them.

Here's a parallel. I'm a Northwestern fan, too, the underdog trying to compete in the Big 10. But when something good happens at Northwestern, it really gets played because there are Northwestern journalists all around the nation. So when they go to the Rose Bowl in 1995 it becomes a huge national story because they have a lot of national journalists.

If K-State makes that same run, it doesn't become a national story until it gets three notches higher. They are not sitting there with K-State grads in production roles or in a producer's seat at the national television networks. It's always an uphill battle.

Many fans will give you basketball stories of the immense pride they had in having a national basketball program. They were a Top 25 team from the 1947-48 season to 1988. They were always right there.

They had been so-so in the Big Six. After World War II, Jack Gardner built that program. Kansas State had this guy who was challenging Phog Allen, going toe-to-toe with him. Then came Tex Winter and he had the Bob Boozer teams in 1958-59. Then it rolls into Cotton Fitzsimmons for two years and then to Jack Hartman. It just keeps rolling and rolling.

They were a national story, No. 1 in the country, and played for the national title.

The "Gettysburg game" was the Kansas game in 1988 (for a spot in the Final Four). That was the game that spun it 180 degrees. If K-State wins that game and goes to the Final Four in Kansas City, it would have been their first visit to the Final Four since 1964 when they were in Kansas City.

Who knows what would have happened? There was no Danny Manning (on the K-State roster), so they might not have been able to win it. But the perception would have been that they were a national program. They were on the cusp of doing that, anyway.

What you saw in the 1990s in football was the 1950s, 1960s, 1970s, and most of the 1980s in basketball.

They are a wonderful lot, these K-State fans. You want them as family friends. You want them as business partners. They are loyal. They are passionate, and they are resilient.

LYNN DICKEY
Overland Park, Kansas

Dickey played quarterback for the Wildcats in the late 1960s, engineering a 59-21 victory over Oklahoma in 1969. He has witnessed how K-State gets in the blood of athletes who play at the school.

It is amazing, kind of bordering on a cult, and here's one of the best examples I can refer to.

Just look at Michael Beasley. Michael was just there for a year. But I have heard him make comments about how much he loves Kansas State. I think: "That's weird." The guy grew up on the East Coast, a big city kid. He's one-and-done in Manhattan, and he's now living in Miami and making lots of money. But if you ask him, he loved it.

There is something cultish about that. He's a kid who was there one year and you ask him about his university: "I'm K-State." There is something there, a passion at that university like I have not seen many other people have for their universities.

I hear a lot of people say they had moved here from another state and are big KU basketball fans. But you don't see that about K-State with people who move in – even in Bill Snyder's heyday when they were winning 11 games a year. I don't know anybody who would say they are big K-State fans if they have nothing to do with the university.

It seems like you always had the hard-core guys, my age and a couple of years older. But all my daughters have gone through K-State and one son-in-law. There are a lot of younger people, and they still have the passion.

I see a lot of similarities to the Packer Cult. There is a passion there for the small town. Green Bay is a small town by NFL standards, and there are more closet Packers fans all over the country than almost any other team. The point is that people do have a passion for Kansas State like they do the Packers. They pay attention, and every time there is a loss, a little bit of them is ripped apart.

KEVIN KIETZMAN
Overland Park, Kansas

Kietzman, who graduated from Kansas State, hosts a sports-talk radio show in the Kansas City area. He interacts with Kansas State fans every day. He interacts with Kansas and Missouri fans, too.

It takes a special person to be a Kansas State fan. You'd better be tough. You'd better be resilient. If you are a fighter, you'd better be able to take a punch.

The hardest part of being a fan is being a fan in Johnson County. That has to be the worst place in America to be a K-State fan because you have a gazillion people who have no affiliation to KU who are all KU fans. If you move here from somewhere else, you become a KU fan. If you grew up here and nobody from your family has ever gone to college, you become a KU fan. That's just the way it is.

I think it's because Lawrence is so close, and the basketball team has such tradition. It just wins and wins and wins. And there are just more KU people here, more KU grads. So if you move to Kansas City, you're around them. You make a friend with somebody and they say, "Hey, you want to meet me and we will watch the game?" You do, and KU wins and they go, "Wow, this is pretty cool" and you kind of become a KU fan.

My experience is that you get much past Topeka in the state of Kansas, it is more purple than anything else. Geographically, there is more of Kansas that is for K-State, but not in the number of people.

They are really good people. If I were to paint a picture of the K-State fan base, they are hard-working, honest people who love their school. The old adage that K-State fans have a chip on their shoulder is right. I don't care where you are from, if you are a K-State fan you have a little bit of a chip on your shoulder. Something has you irked.

If you live here in Kansas City it's because KU gets all the attention and they are a little better and it's a little sexier. If you are from western Kansas, you may feel you are a little disjointed because you grew up in a rural area or they make fun of you because it's Silo Tech. Almost everyone I ever met who went to K-State had just a little bit of a chip.

The biggest difference for me in my interaction with the fans – and I am not trying to knock on KU – is when Kansas State blows it and the audit comes out (in Spring 2009) and they have blown all this money and everything. Every Kansas State fan is completely embarrassed. They see it and understand it. They want to read about it. They want to know about it. They want action against the people who did things wrong.

Most typical Kansas fans still don't know their school was on probation for three years when they won the 2008 NCAA championship (for lack of institutional control). They just don't pay attention to that news.

I don't know if that is good or bad about K-State fans. Maybe we wallow in it a little too much. Maybe we should take a lesson from some of these other fans to not pay atten-

tion to the bad stuff so often. It might be good for our men-
tal health.

MAX URICH
Manhattan, Kansas

Urich was Kansas State athletic director from 1993-2001,
presiding over the rise of football and the transition of
Kansas State into the Big 12 Conference. Urich remained in
Manhattan following his retirement.

Dick Towers (former K-State athletic director) told me
when I came here: "Max, if you stay here for two years, you
will stay here the rest of your life."

I just laughed at him. This isn't my school. I have seven
schools I have fond feelings for because when you work at a
place, you feel you are a part of it.

But Dick was right.

The fans here are grass roots fans, loyal to the school first
and loyal to the teams next. I may have known that intellec-
tually as soon as I got here, but I felt it strongly at the
Copper Bowl. The people that went ... this was their deal.

They didn't want this ride in Camelot to end and wanted
to extend it as long as possible.

I had been nervous about how many tickets we would sell.
Not only do you have to have a good team to get invited to
better bowl games, you have to have a great fan base who
love their school and will be enthusiastic and will come
across to the general public as a whole bunch of sophomores
– they know their way around a little bit, but they are still
enthusiastic, still hungry. That grew all year.

We had always had the core fans. But we had a lot of people who jumped on the wagon when our football team got

good, and I am sure glad they did. They became fans once we won. People want to be associated with a winner.

Someplace along there in the late 1990s we had to get away from that "greatest turnaround" thing. I think our fans have gotten away from that. I think the generations have changed, and they are not worried about being a flash in the pan.

This is a new Kansas State. I think their feeling is that we earned it in a new landscape in the Big 12. They are not going to get drug back and reminded that they aren't worthy. They are worthy. I think if we have an off year, people just think about it as an off year and that we will be all right and we will be back.

We lost some fans in basketball during those years, but not because football was successful. Basketball was mediocre, and basketball fans at Kansas State are sophisticated. I also think it didn't bother them that much because, after all, they had football going.

Next to a great quarterback, the next thing that can make a difference for a program are great fans. A great quarterback can put the team and the fans and the athletic department on his shoulder. Fans can do it equally.

STAN WEBER
Overland Park, Kansas

Weber was a player when the Wildcats went to their first-ever bowl game and has been a broadcaster since 1987. His wife has two degrees from K-State, his daughter is attending K-State, and none of his children have any red and blue clothing.

Kansas State is about the people. When you get into the Manhattan area, the No. 1 thing that K-State students experience is the connection to the people in Manhattan. That reaches out a little further to the K-State fans that come into the games.

There is a continuity to them, a love of the university, a love of the state of Kansas. They are rock-solid, hard-working, down-to-earth, humble people. And they really support their team, win or lose.

I could look up in the stands as a freshman, and you could see people enthusiastic about what was going on even though they had not seen much winning. There might not have been 50,000, but there were 30,000 of them who had a real passion. It was something magical in my mind because that was happening even though there was not a lot of hope we were going to knock them dead on the football field.

If you didn't feel their passion at the football field, you definitely got the full feeling of it in basketball. I always sat near the top of Ahearn Field House up in the alumni section. So I was up there with people in their 40s, 50s and 60s. I could tell right away, I was meeting real fans, people who had probably been sitting over at the football stadium believing in K-State to the bitter end.

They were coming week after week with pride.

These people are exactly the type of people who make the world go, salt of the earth, hard working. They stick together.

They are also different from the fans at some of the other schools. There is always an unbelievable enthusiasm around football at all schools. The games are giant events. And if you have a big-time, winning team, people are going to show up and enjoy the heck out of a game and have a lot of fun saying, "I got entertained. We won!" and they can go back to their office on Monday and brag about their school.

But there's a difference with Kansas State. They give the players some room to breathe. There is a feeling that the players are human beings, and they are in it together with the players, win or lose.

Man, they want to win because it's a lot more fun to go home. But sometimes I listen on the radio when we are leaving a road game on our way to the airport. When they lose, most of those fans immediately get the other side of the coin. "We weren't entertained. I don't want to go back to the office."

Where I see K-State fans after a loss, there's a disappointment. But it's like their son played in the game. You wanted to win, but when your son comes home, I don't know anyone who wants to berate their son. You feel sorry for your son. It's more of a "Darn, I wish we could have won. I want you to win. I want you to be happy."

That's what I see in K-State fans. They're with them, win or lose. You see more disappointment. They're pained as if their family members are involved.

JON WEFALD
Manhattan, Kansas

Wefald, the president of Kansas State University from 1988-2008, was the man in charge as Kansas State's football fortunes changed. He was front and center, proudly carrying the purple banner.

It's just like anywhere else: If you win, people will come. If you lose, they don't. If you are competitive, even if you are 50-50, they will tend to come but not in the same numbers. It took our fans two years, maybe three, for them to get excited about football.

Then they became fanatics.

Any little criticism, they took great offense at. Criticism is the way life is, but I guess they didn't think it applied to K-State. And probably it was because of the fact that we hadn't been very good in football for so long and all of a sudden we were good.

I think they were fanatics in basketball, but not to the extent that they were in football. In basketball, we were never Top 10 for 10 years in a row.

The football revival of the 1990s made game days special at K-State.

Photo courtesy of Anson "Buster" Renshaw

But during those 10 years in football, we just won game after game. Now we have Bill Snyder back, and people are excited again. Maybe we can get back to where we were.

CHAPTER 2

Old School

**Outstanding basketball,
mediocre (at best) football**

With the exception of the 1934 football season, Kansas State fans had little to cheer about outside the basketball program.

Ahearn Field House, the old barn, became one of the most feared road venues in the country with fans so close to the floor they seemed to be in the opposing team's huddle. And the overhanging balcony proved to be an intimidating sight to opponents.

Top-notch players dotted the landscape: Ernie Barrett, Rick Harmon, Dick Knostman, Bob Boozer, Jack Parr, Willie Murrell, Lon Kruger, Chuckie Williams, Mike Evans, Rolando Blackman, and Mitch Richmond.

Top-notch coaches went hand-in-hand with the players: Hall of Famer Jack Gardner, Tex Winter, Cotton Fitzsimmons, Jack Hartman, and Kruger.

Conference titles were the norm: the first of 17 overall came in the 1916-17 season. And when the Big 8 was formed in 1958-59, K-State won five titles in the first six years of the conference.

The Wildcats were regulars in the NCAA tournament – appearing 17 times between 1948 and 1988. Most of those years, only 24 teams qualified for the national championships. The NCAA did not expand to 32 teams until the 1975 season when it first allowed more than one team per conference to qualify.

The Wildcats reached the Final Four in 1948, losing to Baylor in the Western Regional Finals (the equivalent of today's Final Four). In 1951, the Wildcats reached the national title game against Kentucky.

That season the Wildcats won 25 games and went into the NCAA tournament ranked No. 4 in the country.

Under Gardner, K-State posted a 147-81 record. Following the 1952 season, Gardner handed off the team to his assistant, Tex Winter.

Winter's 1958 team was ranked in the top five all season, holding down the No. 1 ranking for six weeks at the end of the season. His 1959 team finished the season ranked No. 1, and in 1962 the Wildcats were never ranked lower than No. 8.

Winter's triangle offense worked to perfection for the Wildcats, who won 262 games in his 15 seasons at the school. Eight league titles and six trips to the NCAA tournament (including trips to the Final Four in 1958 and 1964) followed. In 1964, the Wildcats lost 90-82 to UCLA, which won its first NCAA championship that season.

Winter's impact on basketball extended far beyond Kansas State. It was Winter's offense that Chicago Bulls coach Phil Jackson turned to when Michael Jordan was winning championships. Winter still tutors the Los Angeles Lakers.

The Wildcats' string of successful coaches extended into the 1970s and 1980s with Hartman, who guided the team to three league titles and seven NCAA tournament appearances. The Wildcats reached the Elite Eight four times (1972, 1973, 1975, and 1981) and had two more trips to the Sweet Sixteen.

Hartman nabbed stars Rolando Blackman and Curtis Redding from New York, lured Chuckie Williams away from Columbus, Ohio, and recruited Mike Evans out of North Carolina.

Former All-Big 8 star Lon Kruger continued the coaching success story, taking the team to the Midwest Regional Final in 1988 behind the scoring of Mitch Richmond. The loss to Kansas in the Regional Final was devastating to the program, and it wasn't long before the landscape at Kansas State changed.

While the basketball program was piling up unprecedented success — it was voted one of the top 22 basketball programs of all time — the football team was broken.

From the end of World War II through the 1988 season, the Wildcats were ranked last in scoring offense and last in scoring defense in an NCAA statistical study. The school had exactly four winning seasons.

In the first five years after the war, when many schools grabbed returning veterans to man their football teams, K-State hesitated. The Wildcats were 5-63-1 during that stretch.

The school went through 11 head football coaches. None left for a better job.

By 1988 the school had lost more football games than any in the country — 509. The season ticket sales had plummeted to just 7,200. The nickname Futility U seemed appropriate.

Each decade seemed to bring a number of individual standouts: Veryl Switzer in the 1950s, Lynn Dickey, Clarence Scott, and Mack Herron in the 1960s, and Steve Grogan and Gary Spani in the 1970s. But the constant was the number of losses that piled up year after year.

For some reason, Proctologists are attracted to Lawrence...

There were just two bright spots in the K-State football constellation:

The "We Gonna Win" years of Vince Gibson (1967-74), and in 1982 when Coach Jim Dickey took the school to its first-ever bowl game. This was after an unprecedented redshirt experiment in 1981 when most of the seniors and many promising sophomores and juniors were held out to build depth.

Gibson's enthusiasm brought momentary hope for the continuously downtrodden program, generating excitement across the state and producing wildly entertaining upsets, such as the 59-21 beating of Oklahoma engineered by white-shoed quarterback Lynn Dickey in 1969. That lifted the Wildcats to a No. 12 ranking in the AP Top 25 with a 5-1 record.

But the Wildcats lost their next four games, and Gibson ran afoul of the NCAA. The subsequent penalties virtually assured that K-State football would remain downtrodden. The school suffered harsh penalties that set the program back years.

The next coach, Ellis Rainsberger, was tripped up by the NCAA for playing two players under assumed names in a junior varsity game, and handing out 43 scholarships when the limit was 30.

Dickey followed Rainsberger, but after the success of the 1982 bowl team, was fired less than three years later, two games into the 1985 season.

Following Dickey's demise, three more years of futility and a 2-30-1 record under Stan Parrish led to the hiring of Bill Snyder.

At the time Snyder took the job, Kansas State had lost more football games than any university in the country.

Other sports were faring much better than football.

The women's basketball teams were nearly as successful as the men's.

Women began playing basketball at K-State in the 1968-69 season, and over the next two decades won six league championships – first in the AIAW and then in the Big 8.

The women played in post-season tournaments 13 times in the first 16 years of the program's existence.

Stars like Priscilla Gary (1982-83), Tammie Romstad (1979-82), and Eileen Feeney (1977-80) set the stage for later successes in the 1990s and into 2000.

In track and field, the K-State men's team had a cadre of middle distance runners including Conrad Nightengale, Ken Swenson, and Jerome Howe, each of whom represented the school at the Olympic Games. Pole vaulter Doug Lytle also was an Olympian. And the women's team had several national champions, including Teri Anderson in the mile in 1972 and Rita Graves in the high jump in 1986.

Women's volleyball also was something to cheer about with the 1977 team putting together a 49-18-1 record, the best in school history.

The baseball team had mixed results on the field, but several players went on to major league careers, most notably Elden Auker. Auker played 10 years for the Detroit Tigers, Boston Red Sox, and St. Louis Browns. In 1935, Auker's 18-7 pitching record was the best winning percentage in the major leagues that year. His submarine-style pitching baffled batters.

Former Kansas State University President James McCain proclaimed that Auker was "the greatest all-around athlete in Kansas State history." Auker won nine varsity letters, three each in baseball, basketball, and football.

Ted Power fashioned a 13-year major league career with stops with the Los Angeles Dodgers, Cincinnati, Detroit, St. Louis, Pittsburgh, Cleveland, Seattle and part of the 1988 season with the Kansas City Royals when he appeared in 22 games and had a 5-6 record.

Two other notable baseball players from the early years have left a lasting legacy for Kansas State fans – one in a different sport entirely and the other on Kansas State's social scene.

Earl Woods, who lettered in baseball at Kansas State in 1952-53, was the first black scholarship player in what was then the Big Six Conference. Later, he became more famous as the father of golfing great Tiger Woods.

Keith "Kite" Thomas, who played with the Philadelphia Athletics and Washington Senators, is the namesake of one of Aggieville's landmark watering holes: Kite's. Thomas opened Kite's Bar and Grille in 1954 after his baseball career was finished.

***

JAMES WITT
Dallas, Texas

Witt is moving back to McPherson, Kansas, from the Dallas area. His house isn't finished, but he can tell you the exact mileage from his front gate to his parking spot at K-State sporting events.

My father was in the Army Air Corp, and it was based at Fort Riley. But he actually lived in the old football stadium where there were extra dorm rooms, and he played for the K-State baseball team in 1944-45. So I grew up with the pictures of him in a K-State baseball uniform around the house. It was those pictures that attracted me to Kansas State.

I grew up in Chicago and could have gone anywhere I could get into school. When it came time to look at colleges, I said: "Dad, I would like to look at this school." I had this romantic fascination that my father had gone there, and I just wanted to see it.

Jim Witt, his wife, Kim, and sons Chris (left front) and Ryne have the colors down pat for Wildcat fans.

Photo courtesy of Jim Witt

We showed up on campus unannounced and went to the admissions office. The reception we got was unbelievable. They were the friendliest people, and their ability to accommodate us and take care of us ... it was like: "Oh, the royalty is here." We looked at some Illinois schools and some in Minnesota, but once we got to Kansas State it really was a family, embracing atmosphere.

I got there Lynn Dickey's last year. It was really a very positive time for K-State football. They didn't have the senior year they thought they would, and from that point on Vince (Gibson) started to slide. Then came the long dark period of life. But I had seen that glimmer of hope during the Gibson years.

The basketball was always great. Ahearn was unbelievable. Here is a story about Ahearn. When I was in graduate school, I had a friend from Maryland who came there. He sort of poo-pooed me that it couldn't be as good an environment as in the ACC. This guy, who thought he was Mr. Easterner, walked into Ahearn and the atmosphere was just explosive. We blew out Iowa (105-67) that night, one of Lute Olson's teams.

I got out of graduate school in 1976, and I let my season tickets lapse for a few years. But probably from 1980 on, I had season tickets because it was the thing to do. It got tough to keep it up when we moved to Texas. The basketball program has been great. The football program, I went those years when it was awful. But I still loved it, and it was just a great experience.

I don't know that I kept going just for the social things. Maybe I was naïve, but even in the dark years, I thought there was always hope. Every year I would think: "We can't be as bad as we were last year." Quite frankly, they proved me wrong many years. But there was always this hope that you were going to be better.

And you had to keep going because you wanted to be there when it got better. And especially through the (Stan) Parrish years, I don't think anyone thought it could get worse – and it did.

But one thing I've enjoyed – and I hate to say that I am not a Kansan having grown up in Chicago – but there is a spirit that is one of perseverance throughout the state. Those western Kansans, there were a lot of things to over-come to succeed in that part of the world. There is a perse-verance and an optimism that next year will be better, we will keep plodding along, and we are going to make it.

That is the spirit of Kansas, that tomorrow will be a bet-ter day. I think that's what keeps K-State fans going.

It wasn't just: "Hey, let's go have a few beers in the park-ing lot." Of course there was some of that. But it was really people coming to those games and believing that it would get better. That's what kept a lot of us going.

When they hired Bill Snyder, I clearly remember reading everything I could about him. And my first impression was: "You know, this one finally makes some sense."

When I first saw him and met him at one of those Catbacker things, there was something there that you had to believe in. He was not Mr. Charismatic. But he was like Mr.

Reliable ... that John Deere tractor that was going to start every day.

> 66 Snyder was like Mr. Reliable ... that John Deere tractor that was going to start every day. 99

This was a guy who really seemed to have a plan. There was not a lot of hype, there was just straight talk. Stan Parrish probably has a great football mind. But there was such a contrast between the hype of Parrish and the guy who just said: "This is what I am going to do."

That first year, my sons, Chris and Ryne, were really little then. We didn't go to the North Texas game. We were on the driveway at our house, washing the cars. It was early September and still pretty warm. I had the car door open and the car radio on and when we won that game we just had this huge water fight. The celebration with those little boys – who probably didn't quite get it completely – we were laughing and giggling and spraying each other with water. We just had a great time.

I don't know if K-State would be where it is today without Bill Snyder. We would probably be in the Missouri Valley now, playing basketball only, if Snyder hadn't shown up.

There are three other games that are also special. I was living in Texas the first time we beat them up in Manhattan; we buried Ricky Williams. A lot of the friends I have down here are UT grads, and they still can't figure us out. It just drives them crazy that this school with the little Podunk budget can come down here and drill them.

And I will always remember the USC game in Manhattan, the night game that we won. That game just had such an atmosphere. I know USC wasn't seen at the time like they are today. There was just such an atmosphere about that night; it was just electric.

But I think my favorite Big 12 game was Snyder's last one. We came from behind against Missouri. Let's be honest – that put a lump in every K-Stater's throat. At that point, he had announced it was his last game. We all knew he was gone. We were down, 17 points maybe, and I didn't think we would come back. But when they carried him off the field, that was a very emotional moment.

I kept my basketball season tickets even when we moved down to Texas, and even in the bad years. There were years when I would only get to two or three games. But I have a brother who went to K-State and some relatives I would give tickets to, and there were times I couldn't give them away because people didn't want them.

I kept them because I am loyal, and in my heart there was always that hope. I think that is the thing that differentiates K-State people. There is always that ray of hope. And I didn't want to give them up because I have decent seats and I was afraid I couldn't get them back when we turned the corner.

I think basketball is back on the right track now. I love Frank Martin. He is not what you think he is. He really is a Kansan, a hard-working guy who has moderate values.

My last embarrassing story. When I was younger, we lived out in western Kansas and would listen to games on the radio before they were on television all the time. During a tight game I would go into the bathroom and lock myself in. I would refuse to leave. But I would yell out to my wife: "What's the score?" She would yell back, "We're up by two." Then I would wait a few minutes and yell out again. I just couldn't bear to be out there listening.

There have been dismal times, but always inside me there was that hope. That's why I had season tickets. It's why I listen on the radio when I can't get there. You get attached to it. Some people think I am crazy.

I am sitting here in my office with my K-State purple shirt with my K-State purple belt on. I have had a really crappy attitude the last couple of days. When I put this stuff on today, my attitude changed. I told a couple of people on my staff: "I'm in my purple, and I feel better today."

I don't know what it is. The purple changes me.

GEORGE SCHULTZ
Coppel, Texas

Schultz's father, William, once made 17 free throws in a game for Kansas State, a record at the time. George himself may hold the world record for speeding tickets in one trip between Wichita and Manhattan.

Jim Witt (l-r), former K-State star Mitch Richmond and George Schultz have big plans for the Wildcats in 2010.

Photo courtesy of George Schultz

My grandmother went to school there, and my mom and dad went to school there. My grandmother was a house-mother at several of the fraternities: Beta Theta Pi, Sigma Nu, Straube House. So we would go up there to see basket-ball games and see my grandmother. We were living in the Oklahoma Panhandle, but we had a Cessna 210, and we could fly up to the games. My dad would always get passes, and we would sit right down on the floor.

It was in Ahearn with the raised floor. And here I was sitting down there and watching Bob Boozer and all those guys play. It was great, always sold out, just incredible. One year, when I was in junior high school, I think we were No. 1 most of the year.

When I came to K-State, I played on the freshman team, and I was on the varsity team for a couple of years. But I didn't play much, so I never lettered. I gave it up for my education. After that I went back and ran a cattle lot (in the Oklahoma Panhandle) for my uncle. Then I went to work for Cargill Leasing in Kansas City and I used to drive down to all the basketball games.

The coaches when I was at K-State: Tex Winter was the coach; Bill Guthridge, who went to North Carolina, left when I was a sophomore; Cotton Fitzsimmons. When I got back to Kansas City there were some really good teams then, too. Lonnie Kruger came along. Then it went to hell. The biggest mistake they ever made was letting Dana Altman go. Once they let Dana go, I said "screw it" with my season tickets.

I had kept on buying them all along, even when I was living in Memphis and Virginia, then Detroit, a bunch of different places back East, and couldn't even get to the games. I would listen to the games on the radio when I could. Several times, when I was in Minneapolis, I would make phone calls and have them set the receiver next to the radio at the other end of the line.

Here's one that people still tease me about. When I was in San Antonio, if I went out and found the highest spot in San Antonio and turned the car just the exact way, I could vaguely get the game on WIBW. In fact, even here in Dallas that's true. I listened to the game that Askia Jones scored 61 points. I was at the house, and it was fading in and out. At halftime I got in my car and drove over to the highest spot by DFW airport and listened to that game.

I don't know how many people have listened to the basketball games in San Antonio. Now I listen to all of them on the Internet if it is not on TV. And my stepdad still sends me all the articles out of the paper. He will cut every sports article out of the Topeka and Manhattan and Kansas City papers and once each week mails them to me. But the past two years I have been going to most of the home games.

When they got Bob Huggins in there, I bet I was the first one to call and get my season tickets back. I was so excited when they hired him. I was listening to his press conference on the Internet, and I thought this was what it was going to take to get us turned back around. I was so happy because I thought they would at least have a chance. They had to do something like that because they needed to do something to shock the world.

I thought K-State was never going to get it turned around. I didn't think I would see it in my lifetime. I thought they were done. I told that to Frank Martin. I knew it could be done, I mean, good gosh, look at what football has done. I think Frank is going to do great. You can't win if you don't have the players, and our talent level had gotten so bad it was pitiful. But Frank has the recruiting thing in place. He is tough, but he gets along with the kids very well.

And tell me a coach who wasn't tough. I saw Hank Iba when I was going to Oklahoma State. He was unmerciful. I saw Jack Hartman, he was the same way. If you were in his doghouse, it was awful.

The thing that hurt K-State was that we had that drought in the late 1980s and 1990s. That is when basketball was getting real big on television and the internet. It just became a much bigger thing and more publicized because of all the cable television. Up to that point we were well known by everybody as a basketball school.

K-State was the first school to have tents outside (waiting for seats in the Field House). I promise you that. They were doing it in the early 1960s. They would camp out for a week before the games. What sets K-Sate fans apart from the other schools is the same thing I saw in the basketball games when I was a kid. They packed Ahearn. It didn't matter if there was three feet of snow on the ground, it was packed. The kids grew up with that. If you lived in Kansas and your parents had gone to school there, they just grew up with that.

Most of the agriculture-type schools have that: Oklahoma State, Texas A&M, Kansas State. If you go to a school like OU or KU or Texas, it's not the same. Go to a game at Texas. Even when they played KU for the Big 12 championship in basketball, it wasn't sold out. Part of it is that K-State lets their students sit right down near the action. Other places they have them up high and the people who have all the money sit down low. That takes away from the experience for the kids.

Now, my most embarrassing moment. I bet you I hold the record for the most speeding tickets going from Wichita to K-State. I got four of them one night! I was in Wichita in sales, and I called on this guy in El Dorado. This guy had a huge plant there in El Dorado, and I thought I would just stop by and drop my card off and let him know I would keep calling on him.

Well, he wanted to order something. It was the night K-State was playing Indiana (1980), and they had a really good team. Isiah Thomas was on it, and it was one of their better teams. But I am stuck and have to stay there and do the deal.

> ❝ I bet you I hold the record for the most speeding tickets going from Wichita to K-State. I got four of them one night! ❞

So here I am leaving El Dorado (113 miles from Manhattan) about 6:20 and the game started at 7:30. I was driving 90 or 100 miles an hour to try and get there. When I went through those little towns, I would slow down. But as I was coming out of the towns I would speed up. The first one I got was in Florence, Kansas. I was going 12 miles over the speed limit.

I'm thinking: "I got one, I can't possibly get another one." I didn't go more than 20 miles and at the next little town I get another one. I got one right when I get to the interstate up there by Junction City. Then I thought: "Surely all the highway patrolmen are over closer to the game." And I got another one.

I never got to the game until halftime. I was so mad.

CHARLIE CLAAR
Garden City, Kansas

Western Kansas has been Claar's home his entire life. He was born in Deerfield and raised in Garden City. But he and his wife plan to retire in Manhattan where they can enjoy everything Kansas State in the future. He didn't realize in college that a CPA's tax season would interfere so much with being a basketball fan.

I really became a K-State fan from going to school there. I was the first one of my family to go to a four-year college, and I had developed a liking for K-State as a kid growing up. That's just sort of the way I leaned, and that never went away.

I had been on KU's campus a time or two, and it just had a different feel in the way you were treated and such. This was back in 1971, and like for an awful lot of kids at that time, it was our first time away from home long term. I just got more of a closer family feel at Manhattan. After a semester there I didn't have any interest in changing, and Manhattan is a nice town that fit us well.

I went to the football games in spite of everything. I really don't understand a person not wanting to go. It was a fun atmosphere. The football wasn't impressive, but you had fun with the people and fellow students.

The football team was kind of a comedy of errors all the way through. I remember a game against Oklahoma State when I was in school. In that game, we punted, and the punt came down behind the punter's head because the wind caught it and blew it backwards. And there was one of the Oklahoma State players running for a pass in the end zone. They used to park an ambulance at the north end of the field. He still had his head down and put it right through the back window of one of those station-wagon type ambulances they used to use.

Charlie Claar and his wife, Rebecca, enjoy game days at Bill Snyder Family Stadium.
Photo courtesy of Charlie Claar

Basketball was the other way completely. I would buy a reserved seat for the KU game because I wasn't willing to stand outside a day-and-a-half when I needed to go to class. There was one year we got some people hurt when they opened the doors to Ahearn. The crowd just surged in and just blew the doors off the deal. That's the kind of interest there was for the basketball team.

For the football team, at that point, that was something you just didn't ever see changing. It didn't seem like there was any real pressure to change the way it was. It wasn't something people really talked about. We wanted the program to do better, but nobody … you didn't see or hear any plans to make it better.

We got season tickets, maybe two or three years before Bill Snyder came. It wasn't your best of times. Most of the time, we went (to Manhattan) that day and then came back, even on those 6 o'clock games. We drove back to Garden City and would get back at 2:30-3 in the morning. Today I would tell myself I was an idiot for doing that. But at the time you just look at things differently and maybe don't use some common sense.

For a long time, my wife wasn't really interested in football. She said football, Ugh. No, I don't want to go. Football is dumb. Then we got to tailgating and doing all of that stuff, and all of a sudden you couldn't keep her away. That has grown into the basketball stuff, and now we love everything that goes with the events and the people and friendships we have made.

We got our basketball tickets right after Tom Asbury was fired. By then, we both knew we wanted to retire to Manhattan. I wasn't going to wait to get the basketball tickets and risk that you couldn't get good tickets. So I said we're buying season tickets now, and we will have a chance to move down where we want to be when we get to Manhattan.

When we got the tickets I hadn't been to many basketball games in Bramlage, which is terrible. But I didn't know if they numbered from the top down or the bottom up. The tickets said Row 1, seats 9-10 in Section 5. I called and asked if the tickets were where I thought they were. Carol Adolph, who was in the ticket office at the time, said: "Yeah, somebody gave up some great tickets, didn't they?"

So we're on the front row between the free-throw line and midcourt. The first game we went to we had tickets right next to a life-long friend of mine, Marc Miller and his wife, Lucinda. Marc and I were born 16 days apart in Deerfield. Neither of us knew that the other had gotten tickets, and here we were sitting next to each other at the basketball games.

Boy, there are so many memories, but probably the one that sticks in your mind after everything was the game with Nebraska when we beat them at home ... the snow on the field ... that was a long , long, long time coming. You could see the kids' desire to run down and get on the field and fill it. It was fun to watch that. And up in the stands, we were just wasted. You had put everything into it, the same as the players. You were just beat. You had worked pretty hard at trying to help out with what you could do. And you were: "Great. We finally got that done."

A close second was the OU game in Kansas City (2003). On the way up, you would stop in a restaurant or a filling station on the way up and you would hear this "Boomer Sooner" hollering and shouting. We got so tired of that, and when they blocked that punt, you were thinking: "Oh boy, here we go again." But when it turned around and we were heading home on that Sunday, those people weren't even talking to each other in the rest stops and restaurants.

Part of the enthusiasm is that we were long-starved. That obviously contributes to why we have gone to bowl games traditionally in bigger numbers. It was so long when we never had anything of that nature and had never gotten to participate in it. And with the family feeling, I think you do more things like that because it's doing another thing with your family. You want to know and see and be aware of K-Staters. If you see another Powercat car coming at you, you wave.

I don't see that with our KU friends. It's not the same reason they go to the games, and when you talk with them you don't have the same discussions about the games. I don't think the difference is bad. It works fine for them. The family feeling fits better with most of us.

I am involved with the Alumni Association, and we were going through the process of interviewing groups about Kansas State and their feelings about the school. One of the comments we got really sticks with me. This person said: "You know, when you come over the hill and you first see Manhattan and the general area, you just get this feeling that you are back home."

That's kind of a neat way to look at it.

LYNN DICKEY
Overland Park, Kansas

Thank Dickey's mother, Ethel Josephine, for the Wildcats' 59-21 win over Oklahoma in 1969. Without her, Lynn might never have come back for the second semester of his freshman year and wouldn't have become the purple fan he has over the years.

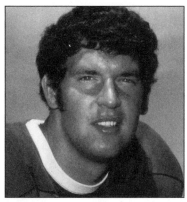

Photo courtesy of K-State Sports Information

When I got to school, I wouldn't say I was a big fan yet. I was a really green kid, and after our four games on the freshman schedule, I was just lost. We became hamburger for the varsity. I was butting heads with offensive linemen in practice, and I remember thinking, "I didn't sign up for this."

At semester I wanted to get out of there really bad. I wanted to go to Fort Scott Junior College where all my buddies were. They were having a great time. I hadn't had a date all semester, and I was feeling really homesick. But the day I was going back for second semester, my mother pushed me out the door on a Sunday night at 10 p.m. She closed the door and locked it. I think I cried the whole two hours back to Manhattan.

Vince (Gibson) had an off-season program, and we started when I got back there. It took my mind off everything else. It was work, real work, and I needed that. The basketball season was going, and I became a dyed-in-purple fan right then. I became a big fan, not only as a football player, but as a student, also.

Lynn Dickey in action.
Photo courtesy of K-State Sports Information

I remember the day before my mom died in 1991, I was sitting with her in the hospital, and we talked about that. She was laughing. I was laughing. She said that was the hardest thing she ever had to do in her whole life, to push me out the door. But she said: "I knew it was the best thing for you." I had no choice in the matter, Ethel Josephine said: "You get back up there Lynny," then she shut the door and locked it.

I had grown up my whole life thinking I would go to KU eventually. My high school coach, Bill Freeman, would take me to K-State games. We had a guy from Osawatomie who flew us in his small plane to watch K-State play football that year.

I was being recruited by all three of the schools; Pepper (Rodgers, at KU) and Vince, and Dan Devine (at Missouri). At the time it was probably KU No. 1, Missouri No. 2, and K-State No. 3.

I remember how KU got eliminated. I was supposed to go to Lawrence on a Friday night to a basketball game for the weekend visit. On Wednesday, John Cooper called and asked if I had made up my mind.

I told him I had a couple of more visits and that I was going to take them. Then he said that when I came up on that Friday, I needed to have a decision or I could forget it.

I said: "Well, you can just forget it now." About a minute later, I get a call from Pepper. He told me he had heard about my call with coach Cooper and said there was a misunderstanding and I should come on up to Lawrence.

I said: "Naw, I'm done."

I had already orally committed to Dan Devine at Missouri. They were a Top 10 program every year at that time. They went to bowl games. But then I started thinking that Missouri runs the option there. Dan Devine kept telling me they had never thrown the ball because they never had anybody to throw the football. I am thinking, all the guys in the history of the program since he has been there and nobody can throw the football? That sounded pretty hokey.

Plus, Vince Gibson had done nothing but tell me we were going to throw the ball 40 times a game. We were going to play a pro offense and throw it. He said he was going to build a brand new athletic dorm to live in and a brand new stadium to play in and that it would be ready by my sophomore year. I thought, "Wow, that's everything I want."

66 'You get back up there, Lynny.' Then she shut the door and locked it. 99

I didn't even think about it at the time that we hadn't won a game in quite a while. What stupid kid would commit and come to a school and not even know they hadn't won a game in three years?

When Vince got there and first started that "We Gonna Win!" and the "Purple Pride," it all seemed pretty corny to me. As a player, I wasn't really buying into that. But the fans did. I still remember women who had gone out and bought those purple wigs. It seemed like a couple of hundred ladies were wearing purple wigs, and you're thinking how crazy can you be. But that was part of their passion.

I'll tell you what: Give Vince Gibson credit. He excited those people.

I got my first sense of the fans from going to Ahearn. That was such a great atmosphere, and they were so raucous and to be a part of that was so good. It wasn't until my junior year in football where the fans got really amped up and got into football. The Oklahoma game is what really triggered it.

When Snyder came in I heard something I had never heard from a coach before. I was at the Royals Stadium club when he was over to talk to people the first time. When you didn't really know how he is the most polite, generous guy in the world, he said something that sounded pretty arrogant at the time.

He made this statement, and he almost got a little angry about it. He said: "I hope all of you who are not buying tickets right now to come to our football games next year, I hope within a couple of years there aren't any tickets and you aren't able to come to the games."

Now this was not a hot ticket. Trust me, you could find a ticket if you wanted to go to a Kansas State football game.

Here it is 21 years later, and I still remember that conversation.

Now, I follow the women's games. When Deb Patterson has her gals out there playing basketball, I am reading the paper every morning to see what happened. Do we root for them a little more because they are small-town Kansas kids? I think that is so cool that there are all these little towns in Kansas, and these girls have come together and are playing with a passion and wearing the purple proudly.

It is very symbolic of the whole university. Maybe it's the small town vs. the world thing.

DAN AND BETH BIRD
Anthony, Kansas

The Birds have not only been great fans of football and basketball, they've been active in the Alumni Association, helping to raise funds for a new art museum. The Wildcat sculpture in the K-State garden is a donation from them. But of most interest to many in the K-State nation is the Purple Palace they live in, where purple rules in every room and there is nary a shred of crimson or blue.

You bring a KU or OU or whoever person in here, and they get kind of hacked off. We have western art and other sculptures in the living room, but we definitely have filled the basement with purple. It's just full of purple.

We moved here off the farm about 11 years ago, and the people who owned this house had sent both of their daughters to KU. They had kind of a blue-colored carpet, and there were a couple of metal braces in the basement that were red and blue.

I told them they could come back and look at the house when we got through with it because we were going to refurbish it. But I warned them the colors were going to change down there. We have a carpet that's purple, purple poles, purple doors, and everything else you could imagine in pictures. Those leather chairs that you sit at the bar that (Jack) Vanier used to provide for the Catbacker auctions. We have them. Volleyball, football, basketball ... it just goes on and on. It's kind of crazy, but it's fun.

Oh, did I tell you? I just traded off a purple Mercedes with 132,000 miles on it. We have a silver Navigator with a Powercat pinstripe. I just got a smoke-colored Lincoln. In the sun it looks a little bit like a smoky lavender color.

I grew up listening to K-State basketball: the Dick Knostmans, Ernie Barretts, that era. All through high school I knew where I was going to school. I played a little basketball in high school, and I went out for freshman basketball. That was in 1957. There wasn't one player off that team that made it to go on. But I had a great time, got to know Tex Winter and Howie Shannon.

I met my wife my junior year. She was at K-State. She was from LaCrosse, Kansas. We kept going to games in our young marriage, and we have had season tickets since Vince Gibson.

Coach Snyder talks about the 13,000 fans who were the foundation of the fan base. Well, we knew every one of them. Things just grew from that. Needless to say, you don't know every one of them now with 48,000 ... 50,000 ... 53,000. But we know quite a few of them. We've had season tickets in basketball off and on, but we started up again in the Huggins year.

I'm excited that Coach Snyder is back, but he needed the time off. The only thing I disagree with him about is that statement he made that he is sorry he took the time off. But he needed to. Now he is really back sharp, healthy. I kidded him about having a pink tinge in his cheeks for a change instead of that drawn look. He's got what I laughingly call the disease. He has a passion for coaching.

That's the great thing about these people who come in here like he did. They don't leave. They fall in love with K-State. (Jon) Wefald worked tirelessly because he loved the people. Same way with Snyder. And (Bob) Huggins, for crying out loud, he knew that he was in the middle of a great fan base. Frank (Martin), he loves it.

We just have such a tough row to hoe to compete with the schools that have so freaking much money. But we turn around and beat Texas two years in a row in football and we beat them once in basketball. So we can compete on the field. These universities that have all this manpower and this money still have trouble competing on a certain day.

The thing that makes K-State fans special is that they've been through thick and thin. They have seen the terrible down years. You'd get cranked up with Jim Dickey, and all of a sudden it crashes. Well, you have been through all of that.

But the work ethic, the people, the students that went there and came out of there, honestly had a work ethic. They are just fine people.

I have watched that and grown up with that. You don't quit. You don't give up. You can get things done with less.

It's an amazing phenomenon. I know other universities come in and try to figure out how we get our funding done. We lead the Big 12 and the Big 10 in the percentage of alumni that contribute, not the amount of money as some of them, but the percentage of the alumni who give back to the university we are pretty proud of.

JIM COLBERT
Manhattan, Kansas

Colbert, one of K-State's most celebrated alumni, is a two-time player of the year on the PGA Champions Tour. He was runner-up in the 1964 NCAA golf tournament for Kansas State. But it was his love of football – bad as the team was – that originally lured him to Kansas State.

I was at Oklahoma State the day I was supposed to enroll down there. I had come down to school early and had been staying with the golf coach, Labron Harris. The football team was practicing, and I went out to watch them practice. I told the golf coach: "I think I will go out for the football team."

He said: "Well, my golfers don't play football."

I called up at Kansas State and asked if they had a football scholarship. They said yeah. So I changed my mind and came here. It was a last-second decision. I had gone to Oklahoma State to play golf, which is what I ended up doing here. But I did play one year of football.

After that one year of football, I went into the athletic director's office and met with Mr. H.B. Lee. I said: "Mr. Lee, is there any chance I could get a golf scholarship to this school?"

He said: "Colbert, now you are getting smart."

What has been important to me about this place is the people at the university and all the townspeople. They are some of the best people I ever met. When you say "Kansas

State" you're talking about the bricks and mortar. It's the people who made it special.

When I was in college, I also worked at the Manhattan Country Club. I played golf, and I was also the bartender. So I got to meet all the people from town. That was the one place to go for all the social functions, and I would work all of them.

I knew the president of the university. A lot of the professors played golf. So I knew an awful lot of people after five years. I always thought the world of the people from the town and the university. We like it here, being around the university and all the functions and all the sporting events. It keeps you young. That's why we moved back here.

We go to the women's volleyball games, I go to the women's basketball practices, men's basketball practice, football practice. I just like it. I think it keeps you young.

When I was here, Tex Winter was the basketball coach, and we had some very good basketball teams. The football ... it was terrible. Then Vince Gibson had a pretty good run. The first time I met Vince, I was in Atlanta, staying at the Hyatt downtown or someplace.

I got a call in my room, and this voice says: "Jim Colbert? You Jim Colbert, the K-State golfer?"

"Yessir."

"I'm Vince Gibson, the new football coach here. I'm in the bar downstairs. I want to buy you a drink, so come on down." That's how I met Vince. He got me pretty actively involved. He had a great run here. And so I was coming back quite a bit during that time.

I left in 1973 and moved to Florida, so I wasn't around too much. I kept following the teams, everybody does. I was coming back to help raise money for the men's and women's golf teams. There were years the school didn't support it at all. I used to bring in the pros for a fund raiser. Fuzzy Zoeller, the day after he won the Masters, he was here.

And of course Snyder got me coming back. I think in his third year, after they had won seven games, he and Ernie Barrett and Bob Krause came out to Las Vegas to raise money, like they do. They met with me and my partner, Ron Fogler (K-State golf coach from 1968-75).

We are having dinner – coach Snyder denies this story is true now, but everybody knows it is true. I had just met him, didn't know him at all. I said: "Coach, you have done an unbelievable job. To win seven games at K-State is unbelievable. You are going to get some really good job offers, and if I was you I'd take one of them. Turn this over to a younger guy and see if they can win 5, 6, 7 games a year because that's about it."

I'm the wise old man, right? So he never forgets that. Two years later, we go to the Copper Bowl. I had been out playing golf, and when I get back to the hotel the team is coming out to get on the busses. I have to stop and wait because I'm carrying my golf bag and of course it's got my name on it.

Coach Snyder comes filing by. He's the last one. I don't think he would have known me from Adam except I am standing there with my golf bag with my name on it. As he comes walking by, he doesn't stop or anything, he just kind of had this little grin on his face and looked over at me. "And you said it couldn't be done." And he kept right on walking.

Well, when we started winning football games, it really turned things around at the university. Kansas State was supposed to be the agricultural school that didn't have any money; they just had a bunch of farmers. The perception was that KU had all the money and we'd never catch up with them.

When we started winning football games, our alumni came out of the woodwork. Besides all the athletic stuff, we have a new library, there's a new rec center, a new art museum. All that became possible under Dr. Wefald, partly because we were winning football games. It's always been a great academic school for years. But the window to get all that out there was winning football games.

Putting 50-some-thousand in the stands is huge for the town economically. And it's huge for the school. All the professors and deans have seen the benefits to build better facilities, get better students, give more scholarships. And it's helped them recruit the best professors.

My connection to Kansas State is pretty well known. I hear it all the time, all over the world. I would be walking to the practice tee at a golf tournament, and a guy might turn to his wife and say: "There goes Colbert. He's a big K-State guy."

I don't care where they are from. They might be a big Missouri fan or a big Texas fan or any of them. It's always "There goes Colbert, he's a K-State guy." And people are always asking where my purple is.

I was just up in Des Moines, and I had gotten a new sponsor and some new shirts. I didn't get any purple ones. It was kind of a rush deal. And that's what I heard all week. People expect me to wear purple at least once a week.

JIM AND SANDY VADER
Prairie Village

It truly is a family affair for the Vaders. Jim was a track athlete at K-State from 1957-59. Sandy was a cheerleader. Jim's brother, Joe, was a football player from 1957-59 and his brother, Jay, was a football player from 1967-69. Their son also played basketball as a walk-on for Jack Hartman.

Back then we were just terrible in football. Then Vince Gibson came in and that's when my brother Jay went there. We helped do all the recruiting (it was legal then for alumni to assist in recruiting) in the Kansas City area.

They won a few games and got successful, and then when they built the new stadium, I bought season tickets. Chairback seats, and we still have them. No fees, no taxes, free parking for lifetime – they never should have done that. But I have never let mine go.

Brother Joe and brother Jay let theirs go. But I kept mine because I felt an obligation that since I got a free education I should keep them, and football is what pays for everything else. It's the best thing I ever got. I have the same two seats I had in 1968 when we went into that thing.

They were losing all the time, but I just enjoyed watching the games. Even when my son was up there, the football team was so bad they wouldn't even go to the games. If I was in town, I would go to every ball game. I had to beg him to go with me, and then everyone would bail out at the half. Even in the new stadium, they were drawing 17,000-18,000 after the Gibson years.

It feels like a family thing. I think possibly that's because it was a small school, and it always was. And I believe a lot of it has to do with the home life in western Kansas. Fraternity brothers of ours were just so proud of it being an agricultural school. A lot of their families were in farming and ranching and cattle. It's kind of a smaller-knit group. And that has a lot to do with the philosophy of why the fans think the way they do and love the school.

When we were in school, the Big 8 (preseason) tournament in the Auditorium was such a social gathering. The kids from western Kansas, a lot of time their parents would give them the tickets, the hotel room and spending money just to come to the old Muny to watch the Big 8 basketball tournament.

Neither of my parents were college graduates, and they wanted me to go to St. Benedict's or Rockhurst. But Moon Mullins, a former athletic director at Notre Dame, was up there and a good friend of several of the people from Kansas State who knew my parents. When the scholarship came through they were assured we would be fine up there. And they became big K-State fans.

I had gone to Ward High School. Sandra was a cheerleader at Wyandotte High School. We were dating at the time, but she was going to K-State anyway, regardless of where I went to college. So we both ended up going there together.

I was recruited and had signed to play football in 1955. But I didn't know I was going to be running as good as I was the following spring. I won the state big-school 440, and I started getting track scholarships. Being the size I was, it wasn't a very difficult decision to make. When (track coach) Ward Haylett said he would give me the same scholarship that (football coach) Bus Mertes was going to give me, I made the switch really quickly.

Hey! I hear KU's a four-year school now!

58

Then my brother Joe followed. People always used to say they took me because they really wanted Joe to come up there the next year. Joe is 6'4" and was playing all three sports.

I had never seen a Big 8 football game in my life, and when I was in high school Harry Deckers kind of recruited me. He would take us up there on Saturday. You would go into the locker room and eat in the training table with the scholarship athletes. To go up there and to think we might be able to go to a school that big, our eyes were big as saucers. I guess I was in awe of being around athletes who we had followed in the newspaper.

Then after I got out I was president of what now is the Catbackers. Back then it was just the Alumni Association that we started in 1961 or 1962. There were eight of us at the Downtowner across the street from Municipal Auditorium. Ernie Barrett would bring that film down and we would watch it. I have been going to and running those K-State Catbacker things for 49 years. I still go to them.

I wasn't really a fan of having Coach Snyder come back, but in retrospect of what has happened, it is maybe the best thing. He has a love of the school so much, and he saw what was happening with Ron Prince. And it is his name up on the stadium.

I will never forget them scoring that first touchdown against North Texas State (in 1989) to win that game. I will never forget that as long as I live. K-State broke that long losing streak.

I think there is a parallel a little bit in the philosophy of Snyder and Jack Hartman. They can take an athlete that nobody else would want – Ed Nealy for instance, or Carl Gerlach would be another – they took guys who weren't heavily recruited. They were good athletes, not great athletes, but he made them great by coaching them. He adapted.

Frank Martin, I am happy with him. He has a demeanor that: "God, you think he is mean." He doesn't smile. But I think the kids like him. So I think the basketball situation is in good shape. It's hard to recruit to Manhattan. It's hard to get coaches to come in here.

BYRON WINANS
Dodge City, Kansas

Winans attended K-State when basketball ruled, watched the transition to a football school, and has hopes that both will be at the top of the heap soon. He was on the athletic council when Bill Snyder was hired as head football coach in 1989.

I will never forget when Snyder is being introduced to us, and we're having a meeting, and we go over to the football office. Steve Miller (athletic director) was there, and there were a couple of others, and Steve was telling (Snyder) how this is a nice deal. Bill didn't really like much about the whole setup, and I thought: "Oh, my gosh."

But I sensed something about him. I don't know if I would say to you that I felt like he was the real deal, but I do know this. Right then and there was a guy who knew what he needed. He was saying: "This is where we have to start, and we will build it from there."

It was kind of like he said I'll do my part and you do your part. That's the way I sensed it. I don't think, as a fan, I had ever heard that statement. There was not a lot of hype in him. But he was somebody you could really believe in and buy into his program. He put it to the K-State fans that he would do his part and get the players to play. But we had to do our part and get in there and sit up in the stands.

That probably wouldn't have worked at KU and some of the other places. But we had struggled, had been up to the highs with Vince – the "We Gonna Win" guy – and back down. And you thought that maybe here's a guy who is here for the long term. And the other side is that he was coming in with a new administration that had a little different feeling about athletics.

When we got to that bowl game (the Copper Bowl) in Tucson and played Wyoming, just gave them an awful whipping, that was the game that sticks out in my mind as much as anything. It was the atmosphere, the feeling that maybe we belong, maybe we were going to get there. I actually went to the bowl game in Shreveport (the Independence Bowl in 1982), but the one in Tucson was just what the bowl business was all about with the festivities, the hype.

The Tucson bowl, which kicked off the bowl series for Snyder, was monumental. The fans were into it. Maybe it was our turn. In my mind, it was the release that we had made it. It was the idea of hey, this is great. The fans can enjoy these kinds of trips. They are doable.

I've always sort of been the fan of the underdog. When I was growing up in Newton, Kansas, it was probably a little heavier KU (fans) than K-State. But K-State was a little closer to home. Friends of mine were going there, and I always kind of felt like K-State was the underdog in the state when it came to the teams in the Big 8. That was part of the reason I chose to go to school there.

Once I was a student there, it just got into my system.

After I got out of school in 1963, I was in Iowa for six or seven years. I was transferred back to Kansas City, probably in the early 1970s. I don't know if I had season tickets then, but we went to almost every one of the football games – the lean years.

I guess it's maybe like some people say: "Once a Wildcat, always a Wildcat." It's like you're walking down the street and hoping you'll find a $100 bill. There's always hope. And at the same time, you get to go back and see friends and enjoy things, even though you don't have great success on the field.

During the Big 8 days, there were the haves and the have-nots, and the way I viewed it there were more of the have-nots. I looked at Nebraska and Oklahoma as the haves and the rest of us as maybes or wanna-bes. In basketball, it boiled down to Missouri, KU or K-State. But that old saying: "Wait until basketball" ... That was a saying I never really appreciated – even if it sometimes was the truth.

In basketball, it was kind of like we fell off the edge of the earth. After Lon Kruger left, we just had some difficulty in finding the right guy to run the program. When you are not involved in those decisions, how do you second-guess them? It was one of those things that you sort of feel that once in a while you need a break, and it just seemed like it wasn't our turn to get a break.

Through the 1990s, we lost all the doggone exposure. When games started getting on TV all the time, it could make you or break you in recruiting. That was probably driven home more when (Bob) Huggins was here for a year. The exposure we got made people realize how important it was. In the three short years since then, we have more talent than we have had in the past 15 years. Huggs changed the complexion of the talent and re-energized the basketball folks.

Probably the highlight of the last 15 years was when we beat the Hawkers (KU) in Bramlage. I wasn't at those games we won at KU. But of the games I was there, that would be the highlight game. The thing that was so blankety-blank exciting was that I had given my tickets on the sideline to my son and three grandkids. I was about 15 rows behind. The crowd and the noise level may have been at an all-time high from the get-go.

With about a minute-and-a-half left in the game I began to get the chills and goosebumps just knowing we were going to win. The noise level in Ahearn was astronomical most all the time because when I was in school we were pretty blankety-blank good. It was like the old barn in Ahearn when it is full and the crowd was loud.

I don't think it was who we beat – though maybe it was – but the students were into it. The fans were into it, and that's what it's all about.

GARY SPANI
Kansas City

Spani played linebacker at Kansas State from 1974-77, earning All-America honors his senior season. He is the only K-State player enshrined in the College Football Hall of Fame. He still holds the record for most tackles in his career with 543. His daughter, Shalin, is a player on the women's basketball team.

I actually grew up going to KU basketball camps when I lived in Kingman, Kansas. So I just didn't know a lot about K-State. When I moved to Manhattan after my sophomore year in high school is when I started learning about the school.

Gary Spani
Photo courtesy of K-State Sports Information

It really didn't make a lot of sense for me to go there because they had a couple of young linebackers at the time: Theopilis Bryant and Carl Pennington.

But I just kind of wanted to be a part of it. I was looking at KU, Arkansas, and Oklahoma. But Vince (Gibson) was the all-time salesman. I knew it was a building program, and I was OK with that.

And the people in Manhattan were great. There is a sense of loyalty that is really worth writing a book about. The sense of purple blood in the state of Kansas and in K-State is true. They bleed purple. They really are loyal.

That came to a national standpoint when they first started going to bowl games. The number of people going to bowl games was just incredible. Of course, they had waited a long time for it.

But that group of 20,000 or so people, or whatever it was, showing up to watch pretty bad football when I was there were just as loyal then as they were 20 years later when they were winning big. There wasn't a lot of them, but there was a true sense that they really cared about K-State.

They were people who stuck with you through thick and thin, and you could feel that. You knew they were loyal because they kept coming, and there was a great appreciation of that from the players.

My first year or two we had a decent defense. And my freshman year we had Steve Grogan playing quarterback and we had a little offense. He was willing a few good things to happen over there.

Gary Spani earned All-America honors as a senior.
Photo courtesy of K-State Sports Information

It was the last two years we were pretty pathetic. We always thought we were better than were, but our record never showed it.

I remained a fan when I was playing for the (Kansas City) Chiefs, but it was hard. I had to get points all the time in the locker room when we would make bets. But I absolutely remained a fan, and then with the ascension, that made it as satisfying for me as it was for all those other K-State fans.

When they remained loyal, and then there was a payoff, it really was like a long-awaited birth. There's joy at the end, but man ... there was some pain along the way.

I couldn't get to too many games when I was playing for the Chiefs through the 1980s, and with me working here at the Chiefs, it has been hard because there were a lot of things to do on Saturdays before games. It's harder now because my kids are in some sort of something every Saturday.

I get to more of the women's basketball games than I do the football games. One reason is that my daughter is playing, and it also comes at a time of year when it is my off season here with the Chiefs.

The Snyder era is really what changed me as a fan, meaning I got more involved, got more excited, watched more games, and made sure I was around to find the game on TV. That was the shot in the arm.

So I was a fan, but the Synder era infused all of us to be bigger and better fans, and I have been that way since.

In the last four or five years I've dealt with a lot of K-Staters in the booster clubs. Coach Ron Prince got me involved a little more. And my job at the Chiefs, working to bring other events to Arrowhead, has put me more in touch with members of the athletic department.

There's a loyalty in me that will last my lifetime. I'm a Kansas kid, and that is a part of it. I made a commitment to K-State, and Kansas State has done great things for me.

I think I am one of those guys I talked about when I was playing, the fan who is there through thick and thin.

I am a little worried about how K-State can continue to compete financially with the big boys. I'm pretty optimistic on the playing side of it. But financially, it is hard for K-State to stay in the ball game.

We got a boost with Snyder when the team started winning, but I don't know if you can do that financially again. I hope I am wrong.

STAN WEBER
Overland Park, Kansas

Weber, who was a member of K-State's first-ever football bowl team, is now on the broadcast team for football and basketball. But his life is so intertwined with everything Kansas State that he would have remained a fan no matter what.

Stan Weber
Photo courtesy of K-State Sports Information

I really attached myself to K-State when I was being recruited. While I was open-minded to where I was going to school, everything kept pointing back to K-State. Even when I went on recruiting trips (Kansas and Oklahoma State), the opponent was K-State. So it was in the stars or something.

When I was a kid, I was taken to Lawrence with a family that had season tickets. This family took me to about two games a year, so there was a heavy KU influence when I was watching David Jaynes or Nolan Cromwell.

I was part of that redshirt class (at K-State in 1982). What people don't remember is that in addition to the seniors, there were a number of players who were redshirted along with them. Even though I was getting ready for my sophomore year, I bought into the idea. Then I blew out my knee in the final practice before the spring game and missed all of the 1983 season. There was a difference that year, a belief that we were good. You can't compare it to the 11 straight bowl games with Bill Snyder, but definitely the fans were sitting there with expectations of winning and there were more people showing up to the games.

For me, being a fan has grown from there. When you are a recruited athlete, you really come in as a hired gun. You don't necessarily have a love or appreciation of what you are getting into, and the connection doesn't necessarily have to happen. It's different for every individual.

But I got those connections right away and being a part of K-State got into my blood immediately. In 1983 and 1984, when I ended up being the quarterback, I took great pride in representing K-State. I wanted to win so bad – not for the reasons I had previously in my life because it was a competition and we needed to win. But I remember before games thinking you have to do this for these people who support the program. I wanted to win for myself and for the people who had been sitting in these stands for 20 or 30 years.

Yeah, they had a good time when Lynn Dickey was throwing the ball around the yard. But that was at least 10 years before. They were there through thick and thin. That's what got in my blood. I wanted to put a smile on their face as they were walking back to their car and hope they were proud that we were representing them.

Even if I weren't broadcasting the games, I would still have the passion and involvement and want to follow it. I just have a lot more opportunities to connect in greater depth because I am an announcer than I would have as just a fan.

And my kids are fans. Almost everything they wear has some purple in it. My youngest son is in a K-State jersey about one-third of the time that he is awake. None of them has anything with red-and-blue in it. I would assume that they had been brought up better than that. It's not even an issue.

They are surrounded by a purple cocoon. My wife graduated from K-State with two degrees. My in-laws live in Manhattan. My parents go to every K-State game. Every one of their aunts and uncles is a graduate of K-State.

And a Saturday to them is being at their grandparents' house, hanging out and then their other grandparents come. It's like a family reunion every week. They have gotten the game-day experience. Their enthusiasm level is off the charts.

That's fun for me to see because I've got to have a lot of discipline when I am broadcasting the game. People don't want to hear me cheering. But my kids, they don't hold back at all. They tell me what to do in the Wabash Cannonball. I never get to do that thing where people go forward and back; I don't even know what to call it.

My kids, they know every one of the traditions and how to get fired up. After a game when I have spent hours in the press box, I go out and just getting into the car you begin feeling the connection. Then in only a few minutes I am back over to my in-laws and to sit there and hear all the experiences and have them talk about this play or that play and how loud it was.

My daughter is at K-State. She looked at no other colleges. It didn't take very long for her to decide where she wanted to be, and she loves it. Now I am getting the experience from her perspective and her friends' perspective – another new depth of understanding what is going on. I hear first-hand what the experience is like in the student section.

HOWARD SHERWOOD
Wichita, Kansas

Sherwood can't remember ever being colder than he was at the Independence Bowl in Shreveport, Louisiana, in 1982, so he was more than happy when the Wildcats rose in the 1990s and he could be K-State proud again – at warm-weather bowl games.

I don't think anybody was convinced the first time we heard they hired Coach Snyder. He was just another coach, a no-name coach almost. I don't think anyone had an idea – even Wefald, as much as he says he knew it was going to happen. Snyder was just another coach nobody had ever heard of before.

So I can't think anybody really felt like this was going to be a turnaround deal. If they say that, I guess I would question their sincerity. We had been having coaches for three or four years and then you would start over again. That had been the history ever since Vince Gibson left.

We had been downtrodden for so long, it seemed like everybody was kind of resigned to it and lived with it. We even laughed about it among ourselves because we had lived with it so long. But oh, my gosh. When we had a chance to pound our chests, all of us could smile again without having to say anything at all.

We were all hanging on to it and riding the wave and cherishing those successes. It brought a real sense of pride in the university that really hadn't been there. You were always proud of your school, but until then there wasn't too much to be proud of in the athletic arena. Basketball was good, but it wasn't to the heights it was when I was there in the 1950s and we were ranked in the Top 10 every year.

I don't know that I had season tickets every year; I probably couldn't go that far. You know, up until Snyder you didn't need season tickets. If you had an open Saturday and you weren't out playing golf or hunting quail or pheasant or something, you went to the game and walked up and bought a ticket. That's just kind of the way it worked.

I graduated in 1956, so that takes me back a long way. My folks went to school there. They met there in the 1920s. I grew up knowing I would be going to Kansas State. I had two brothers who followed me there, and I have a son who graduated from there. So we have several generations.

Back then we were known as a basketball school, not a football school. Of course there was a spike or two with Vince (Gibson). The stadium came through at the same time, so there was a spike and interest in those 3-4-5 years when we thought it was the real deal. We got a chance to hammer OU a couple of times – once really good. And we were competitive. Then you feel it again about 10 years later with (coach Jim) Dickey.

There was another resurgence of pride when Bill got the thing turned and some enthusiasm and the crowds that went to the bowl games. People still talk about it. Heck, the new athletic director, I don't know if you have had a chance to meet with him or listen to him. One of his stump speeches now is that when he went to the Cotton Bowl and saw the 50,000 K-State fans, he says he knew there was something special up there.

We have season tickets. The week-day (basketball) games are a little difficult unless we are playing KU or Missouri or somebody. When the directional schools come in from Louisiana or somewhere, it's a little hard to get there. I think we have eight; I guess we have more than eight. We use them and share them with our friends.

MARK DOBBINS
Olathe, Kansas

Mark followed his sister, Becky (also a basketball player), to Kansas State. He was a member of the Wildcats' last really good team – the one that reached the Elite Eight in 1988. He also remembers when televised basketball games were a big deal instead of the norm.

When my sister committed to play for Coach Lynn Hickey and went to K-State to play basketball, that's when I really got sold on K-State. We would go up to visit her for basketball games and stick around for the men's games. There was just nothing like Ahearn, even when we didn't have very good teams.

I can remember when Oklahoma came in one year and they had Waymon Tisdale and Tim McCalister. I can remember Eddie Elder had 30 points, and K-State lost the game. But I can also remember thinking that if a fan base ever was going to hoist a team to victory, this was the place. It was and it is.

My family were all Oklahoma fans. I grew up an Oklahoma football fan as a kid. My parents grew up in Oklahoma, and both of their families lived in Oklahoma. I was actually born and raised in El Dorado (Kansas), and I can remember there was quite a K-State influence there. There is a longtime high school coach there, Gary Melcher, who played football at K-State and he was always a positive K-State voice there.

I was playing football and basketball, and I was much more heavily recruited for football. But as I grew older, I started enjoying playing basketball more, even though most of the people around me thought I had a better future in football. But I started going to camps at K-State, and they offered me a basketball scholarship. It was a no-brainer. Everybody around me was saying what a tough decision I had, football or basketball. It ended up not being tough at all.

The way they played under Coach Hartman fit my skill set. I felt I could be successful, and I wanted to play basketball. When I got there I realized it was going to take a lot of hard work. I redshirted my first year, but it was a joy to play for him and learn from him. That served me well down the line. We weren't very good in a couple of those years. Then Coach Hartman had his heart attack, and there were a lot of things unsettled.

When Coach Kruger came back, it just clicked. Steve Henson came in, Mitch Richmond, Will Scott. It just breathed fresh air into the whole situation right away.

My senior year was the first year in Bramlage. Bramlage, today, doesn't get its due as a place that can be intimidating. The Purdue game was the first game to open Bramlage. We had just beaten them the year before to go to the Elite Eight. They came in and they were out for blood. Our crowd was awesome. There were several games that year where our fans were awesome.

When you tell people five years ago that Bramlage can be intimidating, they say: "What?" I said, listen, you have to understand. The crowd follows the team. When the crowd gets behind a team, you can stick them wherever you want to stick them and it's going to be tough. Kansas saw this a couple of years ago at Bramlage. When the game means something and you have a group who can actually do something, the fans come along.

When I quit playing there, I became a fan. But that's the difference. As a fan I am not going to drive two hours to and from Manhattan to watch us get our butt kicked. But I will do it if we have a chance of winning. As a fan, you have an option to be fair-weather or not. I'll be honest: it's a lot more fun to go watch us play when I know we have a chance to win. I am not going to go out of my way to watch us play when I know we are going to get our butt kicked.

It's not going to happen. It may not sound very good, but that's honest.

You ask me about the 15,000, 20,000 fans sitting there in football knowing we didn't have a chance to win. From my vantage point it is called pure stubbornness. I can't come up with any other explanation. We were awful. OK, so you cheer for that touchdown to cut the deficit to 52-7 against Oklahoma.

Is it hope? Is it wishful thinking? Or is it stubbornness? To me it is stubbornness because hope and wishing don't get you very far in college athletics. When you truly have a chance and the game's meaningful, then it becomes meaningful to the fans.

Football is easier to keep up than basketball. There are six (home) games. There are a lot of people who say I can do this for six weekends a year for my alma mater. I went to every home game in football Coach Snyder's last two or three years and Prince's three years. I have to tell you it was a lot more fun when we were good. It started getting harder to go when you know you are going to get your butt kicked by Missouri at home.

I tried to remain a basketball fan. I am a former player. Yes, I was concerned about what was going on in our basketball program. But have I been to more games the last two years than I went to the previous 15? ... Probably.

There's a lot of romance in saying "I'm a K-Stater at heart" or "I am a KU fan at heart." And there's an element of, if I root for KU and you root for K-State, and KU beats K-State, then I am better than you. That's a connection between Americans and their sports. And you have fans who take credit for what the players and coaches do.

Yeah, the boilerplate response is K-State is more blue-collar than KU. KU has the silver spoon, they get all the McDonalds' All-Americas. They get this, they get that. It's all handed to them. Well, I have news for you. I played against KU. They had dang good teams, and they played hard.

I think there is a little bit of propensity for the K-Staters to want a crutch to lean on, maybe.

E.C. BROOKOVER
Garden City, Kansas

One of the things that pointed E.C. toward Kansas State was the love of his 1967 Chevelle and his father's insistence that he return from Arizona to the Midwest. He hasn't regretted it for a minute.

Now that I have a few years, I better understand where my father was coming from. He was correct about staying in Kansas and going to school here, just by virtue of the people I have continued to have friendships and relationships with. He was spot-on. I thought he was abusing me, but he was right. I had no idea at the time why he was being that way.

I had graduated from high school in Phoenix and absolutely fell in love with the area. I had the opportunity to go to Phoenix College and possibly wrestle on a scholarship. He just kind of "hoo-hooed" it. He assured me that was not going to happen, that I was going home, and the car I was driving – which was the love of my life at the time – would be coming home, as well, because it was titled in his name.

So he bluffed me, and it worked. I came home and moved back into the house with him and my mom. He and I talked about college periodically, and he continued to assure me that Arizona was not where I was going to school.

He had gone to Kansas State, but he wasn't necessarily shoving Kansas State down my throat as much as just somewhere in the Midwest. We went down to the last hour in August. I had missed enrollment, and ended up enrolling here at Garden City Junior College. I went two semesters here and continued to live with my parents. After that I was willing to go about anywhere.

I had gone up and attended games in the old stadium and basketball games in Ahearn. It was pretty difficult to be a K-State fan if you were a fan of football. It became more of a reason to go somewhere. In western Kansas, we always looked for places to go.

I guess I didn't get season tickets until probably the mid-1980s. My father always had his, and at times I would have the opportunity to use his. When I graduated I couldn't afford it at the time, anyway. It was great fun through the Gibson days for a short period of time. That didn't last long. I give Gibson a lot of credit. It was because of him that they were able to build a new stadium, so he helped with the foundation without a doubt. And it was then that we thought, at least, it could be done.

Once it got going in the early to mid-1990s, it was a lot of fun. It's a huge difference now. When I was growing up and attending games with my father – this would have been the post-Gibson era – we wouldn't leave the Ramada until 15, 20 minutes before game time. You would just drive in, park, and walk into the stadium.

So it's not only the number of people, it's the enthusiasm they have brought with them. It became such an event, the tailgating, the people getting there early in the morning, it was just such an event.

I don't know what makes Kansas State fans different. I haven't thought about it. It might have to do with the Ag backgrounds, the rural backgrounds of so many people proportionately. I know that whenever we've traveled to bowl games, or even away games, I've really noticed the camaraderie before the event, during and then after. Even if it was someone you didn't know, as long as you had purple on, you were welcome.

We even have several families from here in Garden City who didn't have any relationship with the school, and they got caught up in it back in the Vince Gibson days with various groups of people going up to Manhattan for the weekend. And without a doubt they got caught up in Snyder's success in the mid-1990s. Their kids went to Kansas State, so they started attending events to go up and see the kids. But even after the kids graduated, they attended.

Vince and Dale Carnegie

E.C. Brookover's uncle Forrest never attended Kansas State. He stayed at home and worked on the farm while E.C.'s father, Earl, and uncle Paul both went to K-State. But Forrest was a key player in the early steak fries K-Staters had to raise money for the school.

Vince Gibson was speaking in Scott City, Kansas, and then-athletic director Ernie Barrett told Gibson to make sure he acknowledged Forrest Brookover for his efforts in putting the event together.

So Gibson got up to speak, and as he frequently did, got wound up extolling the virtues of Purple Pride. Barrett was afraid Gibson had forgotten the plan, but as the speech crescendoed to its conclusion, Gibson shouted out a special thanks to "Trees Overbrook" for putting on the steak fry.

"Gibson had apparently just taken one of those Dale Carnegie courses about memory hints," E.C. Brookover said. "Scott City, being a small community and everyone knowing Forrest, got quite a hoot over that. The nickname stuck, and everyone referred to him as 'Trees' from that time on just to tease him."

A Family Affair

When Ray Letourneau and his wife, Bessie, celebrated their 60th anniversary recently, they were joined by their children and grandchildren: three generations of Kansas State fans.

Ray has the longest, most involved history with Kansas State, of course. He was president of the Wichita booster club in its early days. Vince Gibson was a visitor in the backyard of his home, where the post holding up the basketball goal was painted purple and the picnic table had the same hue.

Don Calhoun, who played at Wichita North before playing at Kansas State from 1971-73, was a guest in that backyard.

When Kansas State was looking at its options in the design of Bramlage Coliseum, Ray made several trips around the country to look at arenas so he could make an engineer's recommendation to Kansas State.

Ray had tickets to Kansas State football games before the construction of KSU Stadium, and was the original holder of the same 12 tickets throughout the stadium's history until the last of the tickets were passed on to their children in 2009.

The celebration of their 60 years of life together wasn't about Kansas State.

But you can bet that some time during that afternoon, a little discussion of the upcoming football season slipped in. And it didn't matter that it was an anniversary for the Letourneaus.

The names could be changed to any other involving a family with generations of Kansas State fans. Inevitably, there will be a Kansas State story, and one will lead to another – whether it is a favorite tailgate, a favorite road trip, a favorite game or player.

Ray Letourneau Jr., Kevin Letourneau, Kent Letourneau, and his son Jacob, Dennis Keffer and his son Scott, gathered at Kevin's home in Prairie Village, Kansas, to share their stories.

The Letourneau family tailgates regularly at K-State football games.
Photo courtesy of Renee Keffer

RAY: We sang on the Vince Gibson show.

KEVIN: We sang "Willie the K-State Wildcat."

RAY: One of our cousins who lives in Manhattan did "Willie the K-State Wildcat" words to the tune of "Rudolph the Red-Nosed Reindeer." The first time we did it was at one of the booster gatherings in Wichita. And they had us on TV. Then we were actually at the football banquet and sang it.

KEVIN: I wish we could find a tape of that somewhere. We could still sing the song for you, but we are not going to do it right now. We all had the same outfits on and sang this stupid song.

KENT: That probably was when I was like three or four years old.

GROWING UP

KENT: When we were going up when I was little, like in the 1970s, we would have the whole parking lot to ourselves.

KEVIN: We didn't even tailgate back then.

RAY: We would go out to eat after the game, at Valentino's.

KENT: In the 1980s, we would tailgate before the games and then go out to eat. A few of my college friends that were really diehard K-State football fans would still go when we were terrible. I remember at one of their tailgates when we got good they said: "Sometimes I wish we weren't so good because then we could just roll right into the parking lots and there wouldn't be these crowds and we could go and eat after the games. Now everything is a hassle."

DENNIS: Now you have to be a big donor to get the rights to buy a parking spot. Their parents literally parked right beside the fence. Then they moved them back.

KENT: When we would go up to games in the early 1970s, we would go down to the locker room because dad knew the coaches. That is my early memory. This is so cool because we got to see the locker rooms, go up in Vanier or whatever it was called at the time.

DENNIS: Remember how we all used to pack in from Kansas City in one car? We had to save money on the toll. Whoever drove, everybody else would pay for the gas, but that person would drive. We were sardines in the car.

KEVIN: Now we all drive. Gas is $3 a gallon and we're all driving.

RAY: We're all driving SUV's.

DENNIS: I have laughed about that many times, how many of us were crammed in those cars.

KEVIN: I used to have two purple cars, and the dog was named Aggie. My bathroom is a K-State bathroom down there. I am easy to buy presents for. Buy something purple.

DENNIS: That's what's been cool about being a K-State fan. You went to games expecting to lose in the early days. But you always thought that maybe OU is going to look past us, and we could bite them in the rear end.

KEVIN: We were so bad, that we were just rooting to beat the point spread.

RAY: We would. If we beat the point spread, we considered it a win.

KEVIN: When we were going, we would pull up at game time, park in the front row. All the kids ... these guys were running around the front row back and forth, nobody was there.

RAY: There were times there would be 10,000 people there. And if it was cold, half of them would leave.

KEVIN: All of a sudden it got better and better; people had to sit in their seats.

KENT: One time we talked about going back and figuring out how many points were scored against us in the games my dad saw so we could say, hey, you saw that many points scored against us!

THE GOOD GAMES

RAY: I think that 1998 Nebraska game was my coolest game.

SCOTT: I like the one when it was snowing when we beat them (2000).

KEVIN: I like the snow game, the "Throw in the Snow" game.

RAY: The 2000 game was just awesome.

DENNIS: And the facemask was just awesome. That was Dirk Ochs wasn't it?

RAY: No, Travis got him.

KEVIN: What do you mean "got him?"

DENNIS: Hey, there was no penalty.

KEVIN: There was no call.

DENNIS: I didn't see anything.

KEVIN: Kind of like the Cardinals and Royals.

KEVIN: The Big 12 championship game ... the one we won ... that was huge.

DENNIS: Great quote in that Oklahoma championship game after Oklahoma had marched right down and scored a touchdown. These OU fans were sitting in front of us and they turned and said: "This is just too easy." That was the last points they got. That was sweet.

BAD GAMES

RAY: How about games you remember on the bad side? Austin Peay. You remember that one. This was a close game. We were ahead 22-19. At the end of the game they had a long pass and the receiver was wide open and he dropped the ball. So you are thinking: "Good, we are still going to win." Next play, same play.

KEVIN: Wide open again.

RAY: Touchdown.

DENNIS: And the guy humping Willie the Wildcat at midfield after the game. That's emblazoned in my mind. I'm thinking: "You are not, in front of all 50 of us in the stands, doing that. That's why we changed the logo."

RAY: That was the game I remember.

DENNIS: Thanks for bringing that one up. I have tried to blot that out of my memory.

RAY: Or how about the year we were ahead of Oklahoma and we stopped them late in the game. All we had to do was catch the punt and kneel down and we would have won the game.

DENNIS: The game with all the onside kicks.

RAY: We didn't even need to catch it. The guy ran up to try and catch it, fumbled it and they scored. All they had to do was leave the ball alone.

RAY: Or Louisiana Tech, we were up 28-0 in the first half and lost. That was Air Parrish.

DENNIS: You have to go back to another disappointing loss, the one in Tulane. We had the game won and all you have to do is kneel down. The defensive coordinator leaves the press box to go down and celebrate with the team. By the time he gets to the field we have lost because we didn't have a defensive coordinator when they got the ball back.

RAY: They just drove down the field.

KENT: The other game I remember that was a loss was the year Barry Sanders played.

ALL: Oh yeah, yeah.

KENT: There weren't all the stat boards at the stadium, and we were counting yards from the beginning: "He has 300, he has 320." Whatever he had. I played against Barry Sanders when we were younger. I peaked at age 11.

THE BOWL GAMES

RAY: I remember my dad brought a sign to the Independence Bowl that said "Undefeated in Bowl Games." He pulled it out right at the beginning of the game.

KEVIN: I didn't know that.

KENT: I think my favorite bowl game was the Tucson game (1993 Copper Bowl). It was such a party because it was the first.

DENNIS: Remember they ran out of alcohol at the party.

KEVIN: That was a blast. That was one of the best ones.

KENT: They had a big pep rally at a hotel ballroom. They had no idea how many K-State fans would show up and we were shoulder-to-shoulder, screaming.

DENNIS: Chad May went up there and the only thing he could think to say was we're going to kick their ass.

DENNIS: We didn't go to the next one (Aloha), but we were watching with all our purple. That was a crappy Christmas. After losing that, it was like "let's go home." It was worthless. The Cotton Bowl was a lot of fun. We all went down there.

KEVIN: We didn't go to the Holiday Bowl.

DENNIS: Was that after the Aloha? The quarterback got knocked out of the game.

RAY: Miller got hurt.

DENNIS: Who was our backup?

RAY: Cavanaugh.

DENNIS: He came in and I was real excited about him until the next year when he was our quarterback. He was terrible.

RAY: He wasn't bad.

KEVIN: They've all been good except for Smargesso.

DENNIS: Smargesso was a stud, though. He pulls a Freeman against KU. Don't you remember, KU had like an NFL defensive line?

KEVIN: They knew every play we were going to run.

DENNIS: We went to the Alamo Bowl. That was fun until we lost. Then it sucked.

KEVIN: All the teams that beat us in bowl games, I hate all those schools. I can't stand Purdue. I hate Boston College.

I can't stand BYU. I don't hate Rutgers. That was Prince. I don't count that one.

THE COACHES

DENNIS: Air Parrish. Instead of run, run, run, punt, we were going to pass, pass, pass, punt. That's what he said in his speeches. We liked this guy. He's funny. Then he didn't pass his first few games. When he was asked why, he said it was windy out there. It was like hell, you are never going to pass because this is Kansas.

KEVIN: Now he's the offensive coordinator everywhere. We were good with (Jim) Dickey. Then after that we weren't very good.

KENT: That's one thing that scares me this year. Even when we were pretty good with Snyder we always struggled with Texas Tech. Now there are five teams that play that offense.

RAY: Well, we are going to be playing a different defense.

KENT: I know, but I am not confident that just because Snyder is back we are going to be able to stop that kind of team.

DENNIS: We don't have the horses yet. But we have coaches who are actually coaching the players.

KEVIN: Not running steps.

DENNIS: I actually liked (Ron) Prince.

KEVIN: You talking about the singer or the coach?

KENT: The coach formerly named Ron Prince.

RAY: He could talk.

DENNIS: There were certain things I did like about him. He had all these coaches he brought in from the pro level, and you thought great, we are going to get a lot of this great talent. He got nothing, and those guys scattered as quickly as they could.

KEVIN: Then we had juco coaches.

KENT: The night they announced Prince was the coach, I had a sick feeling in my stomach. I didn't sleep that night.

KEVIN: It could have been Gary (Patterson).

RAY: Yeah, since we all know Gary, it was really upsetting. Gary was in our fraternity when we were in the house.

KEVIN: He was one of my groomsmen.

DENNIS: It's funny to think about ... that somebody from our fraternity is a head coach at a major D-1 school.

RAY: You never would have thought it when he was in college, never would have thought that. But that's probably true of everybody when they are in college.

KEVIN: Prince could dance down the sidelines pretty good.

DENNIS: I liked Ron Prince, though.

RAY: Why would you like anything about him?

DENNIS: I thought he brought kind of a player's coach mentality. That is what I thought when he came in. I liked what I was hearing about him. It seemed like he was down to earth and he was going to get it done. The offensive line was terrible and we got an offensive line coach. We are going to really build this program again. You watched and watched and watched.

RAY: Wait a minute! He kicked off all the talent.

KENT: One of Snyder's comments when he retired was that this was a good time to leave the program because I am leaving it in pretty good hands, there is a core of talent there. I think he was thinking (Allan) Evridge was a good quarterback; (Dylan) Meier would be a good backup.

DENNIS: My point is I liked it when he came in, and I saw him just decimate the program.

RAY: The joke the second year was he had already hired a coach from Cornell, so he hired a coach named Cornell.

KENT: Yeah, a guy who was a running backs coach by trade and immediately made him a defensive backs coach.

DENNIS: At Virginia they say their No. 1 priority, their No. 2 priority, and their No. 3 priority was recruit, recruit, recruit. So I thought this guy would be good.

RAY: I don't think his recruiting was his worst thing. He was worse as a person than he was as a coach. That's my problem with him. He was two-faced.

KEVIN: When they hired Snyder (the first time) and he came around and talked to all the boosters, he pissed me off because he kept saying you guys need to show up for the games. These were the people who were showing up to the games. We're the ones here who go to the games.

KENT: There were like 30 of us there. It was the fourth time I had been to one of those coaching change things. It was always rah rah. Stan Parrish...we're going to throw the ball. Bill Snyder ... well, you know how he is.

RAY: It kind of turned me off at first. He was talking about you need to come to the game before you win and get people in the stands.

THE PLAYERS

KEVIN: Who was glad Freeman went pro?

RAY: Not me.

SCOTT: I don't think he should have been the starter last year.

KEVIN: I was glad he went pro.

DENNIS: I was glad he went pro.

KENT: I am a little surprised he got drafted in the first round.

DENNIS: I can't believe he made as much money as he did. $3.6 million guaranteed. I hope he does well. I hated when Chris Canty went pro more than I hated when Freeman went pro.

KEVIN: I hated when Sproles went pro (laughter). I was mad when they played Sproles his freshman year and didn't redshirt him. I was mad when they didn't redshirt Monty Beisel his first year, too. Sproles had, like, seven yards his first year. What a waste.

KENT: He got hurt.

OPPOSING FANS

DENNIS: I hate Missouri. Their fans are far worse than KU's fans.

RAY: I don't see them as much.

KEVIN: Remember that year at the bowl game when we were watching Missouri and cheering against them. My dad could not understand why we were not rooting for Missouri. I was like, Dad, it's Missouri. Why would we root for them? He said well, because they are from the Big 12. I said you don't live in Kansas City and have to listen to them all the time.

DENNIS: Who was the quarterback? Corby Jones. The Kansas City contingency was cheering like crazy against Missouri.

RAY: I really hate Missouri. I had a bad experience there.

KEVIN: My KU friends don't know I hate KU fans. I'll say I was misquoted. At least it's not an audio book.

RAY: Where did you guys sit the night we went to the game with (Michael) Bishop at Missouri? They sat us next to the students. Man, it was scary. They were throwing bottles.

DENNIS: We were sitting right there in the wedge, right on the line with the MU people. They are turning around and flipping us off and trashing us. Finally their sister gets up and goes and tells a security guy that it was uncalled for and asked him to do something. So they kicked that guy out of the stadium. He came back later on wearing a different shirt and hat and was still flipping us off. But he wasn't as bad. I remember that one.

KEVIN: The Texas fans are really good fans.

RAY: The Texas A&M fans are really good, too. And you know who is great? The Marshall fans. They were awesome. You go to a restaurant before the game. They would tell you how to get to the stadium and which parking lots to use.

KEVIN: Then they'd say thanks for coming to the game.

RAY: I really enjoyed that one a lot.

DENNIS: That first Texas game when we went down there and beat them. These women were drinking pretty heavily. We were all in our purple. They said: "So do y'all think you are going to win this game?" That's what we came down here for. "Well bless your heart." I remember that big Texan after the game. I thought he was going to squash me like a bug. Big, big guy. He stops right in front of me with his boots and cowboy hat on. He looks at me, puts his hand out. "You guys have a hell of a team. Congratulations. Your fans are great." I am like, "Oh, thank you" and I had to go change clothes after that.

KEVIN: We went to one of those Oklahoma games on a bus. We get there and there are two guys just screaming at us when we get off the bus, profanities. Then you go to Texas and it's, "glad you're here." The Oklahoma fans were just cussing you out.

DENNIS: Missouri fans think they are the Oakland Raiders of the Midwest. They try to harass the players in the hotel and stuff. That's kind of what they try to do. And we had that Thursday night game in Lawrence. I had one bet with a KU guy. He had all his KU crap on and I had on all my K-State crap. The bet was whoever won, the other guy had to wear his stuff to work the next day.

KENT: You mean the blue polo that had the pull-off sticky-back Jayhawk on it? (Laughter). Now that their football team is better, they wear real stuff. But back then they wore regular clothes that you put that little sticky thing on.

DENNIS: Anyway, that's the bet. If KU wins, I'll wear my K-State stuff, which I would have, anyhow. He said "No, I'll burn it if we lose." He didn't even show up the next day.

KENT: Normally you don't go to work the next day. But the next day was Friday. I went to work. I bought like three dozen doughnuts. I walked around the building passing out doughnuts wearing my K-State stuff. I said: "Hey, here's a doughnut. Just thought I would buy them. Hey, how was that game last night?"

DENNIS: That was a fun game. Tearing down their goalposts, even I couldn't believe we did that. And you have to talk about the really fun game when they brought in the KU band on that Thursday night game. The tubas made really cool targets for people to throw stuff at. We are not angels at K-State, either.

KENT: All my life I have heard about how great the Nebraska fans are, how they cheer for the other team and they stay until the end and cheer the other team. That first game we won up there, by the fourth quarter of that game, there were more K-State fans than Nebraskans. And they weren't cheering for us. It's easy to be a good fan when you are winning.

RAY: Although when I went out to dinner that night they were pretty nice. Not one negative comment.

OKLAHOMA AND NEBRASKA

RAY: Remember the Oklahoma game we lost, 75-28. Greg Pruitt and (Jack) Mildren. The next year when we played them, I remember they took out Greg Pruitt and brought in Joe Washington (laughter). We didn't know what that meant at the time. But Jiminy ... he was better than Pruitt!

DENNIS: That was the thing everyone hated about OU. They would beat you 77-14, but eight guys would score touchdowns. Nebraska would beat you by the same score, but their starters would score 70 of them because they were always trying to beat the point spread.

KEVIN: It always pissed you off because they (Nebraska) would never punt.

DENNIS: Fourth and 13 on their 10 and they would go for it.

RAY: And they would make it. What I recall is that Nebraska fans just took over that stadium, and I don't remember Oklahoma fans ever doing that.

KEVIN: Well, they're not good fans.

DENNIS: What was it, Chad May's year? We had the early morning game and basically we made it a Visine Game. Get the red out. Do not sell your ticket to a Nebraska fan because we know where your seats are type of deal. We knew we were going to win that game, just had that feeling. We didn't. But we had that feeling that Chad May could do it.

KEVIN: Weren't they on their third-strong quarterback in that game?

RAY: Of course, when we got ahead they put in the second-string quarterback even though he was hurt.

DENNIS: Wasn't that Brook Berringer, the guy that got killed in the airplane?

RAY: We were ahead of them until about the fourth quarter.

DENNIS: You could see Chad May getting mad because he would start kicking. He said they were gouging him in the eyes and grabbing him in the crotch. But we were almost more mad at him that he was complaining about certain things like that. We were above things like that at this point.

BASKETBALL FANS

RAY: Growing up we were bigger basketball fans than football. Jack Hartman was the coach.

DENNIS: We went to the last KU game at Ahearn when (Kevin) Pritchard made the shot at the end of the game to win it (64-63). We watched him drain a shot that was totally guarded.

KEVIN: Those games at Ahearn were so fun.

DENNIS: And in 1988, Scooter Barry had the game of his life in the Regional. I know you guys hate Scooter Barry, but I could still handle that then. Couldn't now.

KEVIN: Kept us out of the Final Four.

RAY: I don't hate him, but it was kind of an anomaly.

KEVIN: I would rather lose to a guy who was good like Pritchard than Scooter Barry. Pritchard was actually good.

DENNIS: We used to go to all the Big 8 basketball tournaments. In basketball, we used to have parties. They would have a party or we would have a party. Everybody would go over in the middle of the day and drink beer and cheer wildly for the Cats. That's gone. It just doesn't happen any more.

FAVORITE HOOPS GAME

KEVIN: The best game was when we beat KU in Lawrence (1994) when they had just become No. 1. Anthony Beane. That was a pretty good game.

RAY: Probably the Beasley-Walker game. That was a pretty good game.

KEVIN: That would have been a good game. But I wasn't at that one. The game I went to was the one in Lawrence, beating them when they were No. 1. One of my brother-in-law's vendors is a KU guy, and he got us tickets. That game and one year we went to Manhattan when Missouri was ranked real high. My boss was a Missouri fan, and he thought they were going to kick our butts. So he said I'll drive, you guys can drink and you guys can buy pizza and go in the van. Then when we beat them, he didn't even want to talk. They were ranked No. 1. We were all there drinking and having a good old time. He was pissed.

RAY: The Russian game was pretty cool.

KEVIN: The Donnie Vaughn Ugly game (Feb. 11, 1978), throwing bananas. I couldn't even throw them to the court I had been drinking so much. I couldn't hit the court. You couldn't find a banana in Manhattan that week.

RAY: I got John Wooden's autograph that day. He was the announcer of the game that day.

DENNIS: I was still a KU fan at that point. I thought how rude those K-Staters were.

RAY: I went to the game at KU when they were throwing hot dogs at Curtis Redding. That's what started it.

KEVIN: That game when we beat Oregon in the NCAA tournament and were on the cover of *Sports Illustrated*. I went to Mother's Worry and watched that shot over and over and over. That was pretty cool.

DENNIS: The other great game for K-State was when KU lost to Wichita State (1981). That was one of our favorite games.

SCOTT: How about when they lost to Bucknell?

DENNIS: Oh, Bucknell and Butler. I had them ship the T-shirts to Kansas. The guy at the store was saying: "What's going on in Kansas?" Scott was getting threatened at school when he wore the T-shirt.

KEVIN: I wore mine at work. Whenever KU loses a basketball game, it's a good night.

DENNIS: It doesn't help K-State when KU wins national championships.

THE COLOR PURPLE

KENT: When did we start wearing only purple? We always wore K-State stuff, but it might be white.

DENNIS: We had a neighbor, and I was always playing catch or something in the backyard with Scott. The neighbor would look in to the yard. He once asked: "Does that kid own anything that's not purple?" I had to sit there and think, I'm not too sure. I guess there is probably something.

KEVIN: Every August I go to work wearing K-State shirts every day. Some of them might be white.

RAY: I don't have nearly that much.

DENNIS: We graduated from silk-screen sweatshirts to logoed stuff.

RAY: At first it was purple. Then purple wasn't good enough, it had to be a logo.

SCOTT: The last two years, the week of the KU-K-State game I wore a different purple T-shirt to school every day. When I did it this last year, I had a purple jump suit. They thought I was a plum. K-State hasn't been very good, so they haven't backed me up.

> **" Does that kid own anything that's not purple? "**

THE RIVALRY

DENNIS: These three were indoctrinated from birth. I was the other way. My brother was a big K-State fan and I was a big KU fan. He went to KU and I went to K-State. I don't talk to him any more (laughter). I mean you have to sacrifice certain things. Purple is thicker than blood. Growing up, I was that little kid in the commercial on his driveway with the basketball counting down the seconds to make the winning shot. And I was always playing for KU and it was always against K-State. If I missed the shot, I would call foul and shoot free throws to beat K-State. Then I started dating their sister. I was still going to go to KU, but then I ended up going to K-State. Once I got there they would announce the scores. We were getting beat by somebody, but KU was getting beat by somebody else and everybody would cheer real loud, thinking it was great. I thought that was stupid. But it didn't take me very long and I was cheering louder than they were.

CHAPTER 3
Time of Transition

1989-2003 – Football emerges, and basketball
takes a backseat

"There is only one school in the nation that has lost 500 games," says Bill Snyder, Kansas State's new football coach. "This is it, and I get to coach it."

Those words, spoken to a *Sports Illustrated* reporter, marked the start of the Miracle in Manhattan, not the *resurrection* of Kansas State football, for that would imply there had been a *first incarnation* of Kansas State football.

In 1989, the athletic landscape at Kansas State was about to change.

Basketball was riding high, fresh from an appearance in the Elite Eight of the NCAA tournament. But failing to reach the Final Four would have unforeseen repercussions.

The football program was under fire. Average attendance was less than 15,000 per game – lower than the NCAA requirements for a Division I school. The Kansas Board of Regents was considering what to do if the NCAA enforced its rules. Nothing was off the board – a switch to Division 1AA, even dropping football altogether.

"It would have been devastating," Coach Bill Snyder said. "It would have had a dramatic impact on this school, and it would not be what it is today."

University president Jon Wefald, fearful that Kansas State would be expelled from the Big 8 Conference, made the decision to pour money into the program. That, too, would have an unforeseen impact on the athletic program and the school.

But as the 1980s were coming to a close, basketball still was king.

Following the loss to Kansas in the finals of the NCAA Midwest Regional in the spring of 1988, there was hope that the Wildcats could continue to be a force in the Big 8, buoyed by the opening of newly constructed Bramlage Coliseum.

Coach Lon Kruger took his next two teams to the NCAA tournament, losing in the first round each time. But by the 1990-91 season, he had moved on to an NBA job, and one-time assistant Dana Altman took over the program.

The Wildcats struggled each of Altman's seasons as head coach. But the most telling example of how things had changed came following the 1993-94 season. The Wildcats had gone just 4-10 in the Big 8, but were invited to the NIT tournament. They won their first three games in the NIT, reaching the semifinals in New York.

The school administration made the decision to not send the school's pep band to the semifinals or finals. The Wildcast lost twice. Altman, seeing the lack of support for basketball, made the decision to leave Kansas State. Tom Asbury, who had had a successful run at Pepperdine, was hired.

By then Snyder, a tireless worker, had made the down payment on the Wildcats' emergence as a football power, taking the Wildcats to the second bowl game in school history in 1993. That started a stretch of 11 years in which the Wildcats went to bowl games. They even challenged once for a National Championship.

There were new football offices, a new weight room, and new locker rooms. A new field was installed at the stadium; a press box and suites followed shortly. By the end of the 1990s, the Wildcats would have a big-league football stadium.

In 1993, Snyder's first bowl team and the fan following set the stage for subsequent bowl success. The Wildcats were selected to play in the Copper Bowl and more than 20,000 fans – remember there had been just 13,000 attending home games only four years previously – followed the team to Tucson where K-State thumped Wyoming 52-17.

Bowl trips followed to Hawaii, the Holiday Bowl in San Diego, and the Cotton Bowl in Dallas before K-State fought its way into one of the top four bowl games in the country. In 1997, the Wildcats rode a 10-1 regular-season record – the only loss at Nebraska – to the Fiesta Bowl.

There, a 35-18 win over Syracuse with a K-State roster dominated by juniors, set the stage for one of the most amazing seasons in college football history. Snyder used the win over Syracuse as the starting point to 1998.

It proved to be a year for the ages. The Wildcats went unbeaten through the regular season. College football's poster boys for futility ended a 30-year string of losses to Nebraska. They reached the Big 12 championship game, sporting a No. 2 ranking in the Associated Press poll and a No. 3 ranking in the Bowl Championship Series.

A loss by UCLA would catapult the Wildcats into the National Championship game – which is precisely what happened. As word of Miami's upset win over UCLA filtered into the Edward R. Jones Dome in St. Louis, the site of the Big 12 title game, K-State fans began making plans for their trip to the BCS title game against Tennessee.

K-State held a 15-point lead with just 15 minutes to play. And even though Texas A&M was ranked No. 10 in the country, there seemed little doubt the Wildcats would handle them after they had romped through the Big 12 regular season by an average margin of victory of 29 points per game.

The unthinkable happened. Texas A&M tied the score and forced overtime. In the second overtime, K-State faltered and lost, 36-33. The dream season turned into a nightmare.

Bowl pairings already had been finalized, assuming a K-State win over Texas A&M. When Kansas State lost, the Wildcats fell to the Alamo Bowl, fourth in the Big 12's pecking order.

To K-State fans it was adding insult to injury, and that feeling was further prompted when the Bowl Championship Series adopted the "K-State rule" that protects a highly-ranked team from falling to a lesser bowl. Too late for Kansas State, which went on to play a horrible first half against Purdue in the Alamo Bowl, losing 37-34.

While the disappointment in Manhattan was massive, the football team wasn't finished.

The Wildcats played in the Big 12 championship game in 2000, losing to No. 1 ranked Oklahoma by three points, then beating SEC power Tennessee in the Cotton Bowl on New Year's Day, 2001.

In the 2003 Big 12 title game, the Wildcats turned the tables on Oklahoma, upsetting the No. 1 ranked Sooners, touted as perhaps the best college team ever, 35-7. In that game, Darren Sproles wowed his hometown fans with one of the all-time performances, rushing for 235 yards in 22 carries and catching three passes for 88 yards. Add on another 22 yards in returns, and he finished the night with 345 all-purpose yards.

Individual highlights in those glory years included Michael Bishop's second-place finish in the Heisman balloting in 1998, and seven players who were selected first-team All-America by at least three different organizations (punter Sean Snyder in 1992, safety Jaime Mendez in 1993, cornerback Chris Canty in 1995 and 1996, kicker Martin

Gramatica in 1997, returner David Allen in 1998, linebacker Mark Simoneau in 1999, and cornerback Terence Newman in 2002).

Eleven other players were selected All-America by at least one organization, and the Wildcats had 16 players selected in the first three rounds of the NFL draft.

While the football team was reaching unprecedented heights, the basketball team was experiencing uncharacteristic lows.

After reaching the NIT semifinals in 1994, Altman saw that basketball no longer had the school administration's favor and he bolted to Creighton University.

Enter Tom Asbury, who in his second season took the Wildcats to the NCAA tournament. But Asbury, after taking the K-State job, flirted with a West Coast school after one season and fell out of favor with Kansas State fans. Eventually the acrimony – and team record – was so bad he was fired following the 2000 season, never having beaten Kansas in 17 games.

Jim Wooldridge succeeded Asbury. And although he bonded with the Kansas State fans, his basketball teams were no more successful than Asbury's. From the 1988 appearance in the Midwest Regional Finals to the end of the Wooldridge era, the Wildcats were 103-176 in Big 8 and Big 12 games and finished in the top half of the league only three times in a 16-year period.

Only one player, Steve Henson from the 1990 team, reached an NBA roster.

The women's hoops team seemed headed for a similar fate, the record hovering just below .500 through the 1995-96 season when the school had to tap former men's coach Jack Hartman to finish out the season after Brian Agler resigned because of an NCAA investigation into the program.

Enter Deb Patterson and what became a resurgence of the women's program. After five mediocre seasons, the Wildcats broke out in the 2001-02 season with a team that featured three Kansas school-girl stars: Nicole Ohlde (Clay Center), Laurie Koehn (Hesston), and Kendra Wecker (Marysville). That team reached the NCAA Sweet Sixteen.

The following year, the same threesome led the team back to the NCAA tournament and a final No. 8 ranking in the polls. And in 2003-04, the Wildcats were co-champions of the Big 12 with a 14-2 record, again ending the season with a No. 8 ranking nationally.

Patterson became known for taking the best of the best in Kansas. Wecker, Ohlde, and Koehn finished their careers as the top three all-time scorers in K-State history.

Volleyball was something of an afterthought until the formation of the Big 12 Conference upped the ante and all sports became important.

Jim Moore's 1996 team put together a 26-9 record and reached the second round of the NCAA tournament. From 1997-2000, under coach Jim McLaughlin, the Wildcats advanced to the NCAA tournament every year, reaching the regional semifinals in 2000 after a second-place finish in the Big 12.

Suzie Fritz took over in 2001, and in her third year the Wildcats won the Big 12 with an 18-2 conference record and a No. 11 ranking at the end of the season after losing to perennial power Penn State in the regional semifinal.

The Wildcats' track and field team continued to crank out Olympic and All-America athletes. Kenny Harrison (gold medal triple jumper in 1996), Steve Fritz (1996), Ed

Broxterman (1996), Connie Teaberry (1996), and Nathan Leeper (2000), all represented the United States. Multi-event athletes Austra Skujyte (Lithuania) and Attila Zsivoczky (Hungary) also were in the 2000 Olympic Games in Sydney.

Leeper (1998) and Percell Gaskins (1993) each won the NCAA high jump championship for the Wildcats, and 23 different men won All-America honors in outdoor track and field from 1989-2003.

The women's track team won Big 12 Conference championships in 2001 and 2002, and from 1989-2003 there were 22 athletes (including basketball's all-time leading scorer Kendra Wecker) who were All-America.

The baseball team had several notable accomplishments in this era. Coach Mike Clark was selected as the Big 8 Coach of the Year in 1990 when the Wildcats finished in second place. Clark was the only baseball coach in school history to be accorded the honor.

Just two years later, shortstop Craig Wilson became the first-ever K-State player to be selected as the Big 8 Player of the Year. He was All-America and later played on the 1992 Olympic team that won the bronze medal. He had a three-year career in the major leagues, playing for the Chicago White Sox.

The groundwork was laid for future success with the renovation of Frank Myers Field in 1998, but not without a glitch. Because of construction delays, the 1999 team had to play virtually all its games on the road – traveling 17,500 miles in the process. Sophomore Kasey Weishaar was selected as Big 12 Player of the Year.

Willie the Wildcat enjoyed the football program's resurgence.
Photo courtesy of Anon "Buster" Renshaw

* * *

DIRK OCHS
Overland Park, Kansas

Ochs was recruited to play football at K-State after Bill Snyder's second season. His first visit to K-State convinced him that was the place to be. His younger brother, Travis, also played at Kansas State and both remain fans.

When my family moved to Kansas City, I was a junior in high school and I didn't think a whole lot about playing in college. I had little confidence in myself as a football player. I was very hard on myself. I didn't think I was a person who would be attracting any attention from a Division I school.

I think Kansas State was my first visit. I went to the awards ceremony after the season, and I could sense a real energy there. They had won five games that year, so it wasn't anything great. But there was such an energy. You could just tell that something was happening. I compared everything else to that visit, and nothing struck me the same way. I just knew it was the right place for me.

My dad is a K-State graduate. My mom is a Jayhawk. When I was a little kid, I had Willie the Wildcat sweatshirts. While I wasn't necessarily indoctrinated, I was familiar with Kansas State.

When I went on my visit, guys were finally starting to see some optimism. They had come off two winless seasons. Then in 1989 they had the one win. This was in 1990 and it was the most games Kansas State had won in a long time. You could tell the players were starting to believe in themselves. It was a special situation, and you had to be there and feel it to understand the feeling.

At the time I don't think I really thought about raising something from the ashes. Looking back on things, I am very proud to have gone to a school where there was no tradition and to have a hand in creating it. You go to Texas or Ohio State or some place like that – well, whoop-te-do! There are a lot of guys who have laid the foundation for that.

I wanted to be part of something I thought was going to be great. I felt comfortable with all the players. It was just a good match for me.

Sure I have remained a fan. You go through something like that you can't help but have the pride. That's a once-in-a-lifetime opportunity. To go to an established program isn't easy from the standpoint that it still takes a lot of work to get there. It is easy to go somewhere you are winning. But to be a part of something that hasn't been done before, that's incredible.

This was a school where they were talking about getting rid of the program or having it move down to a 1-AA or D-2 level. To really save that, and not only just save it, but have the run of success we did, that is something that will stick with me forever.

I am probably not as rabid a fan as I was. It just tore at me when I was playing if we were struggling or had some losses. There is that competitive spirit in me whenever I go to a K-State game. Today, while it still bothers me, it's not quite as much. I have learned to take things differently now.

> I ran into a Cornhusker fan the other day. Then, I backed up and ran into him again.

A lot of the K-State fans are just very much into the university and want to see it do well in everything. Maybe it's a biased eye, but one thing I notice is that I always see way more license plates that have Powercat than I do Mizzou or KU. I see a few more now that KU won the National Championship in basketball, but I still don't see them as much as you see Powercat plates.

I think it's kind of a testament to fans who are extremely proud of their school and probably would be willing to fight to the death for it.

There are some challenging times right now. The last couple of years were kind of tough. There were a lot of things about the program that changed my perception and that of a lot of the other guys. It was kind of like the whole athletic department had gotten away from what it once was. You want to change and evolve, but it is almost like they turned their back on everything that had been done before. Especially in football.

Last year I had quite a busy work schedule that prevented me from getting to a game. It was the first time I did not make it to a single game, and a big part of that was I had so much going on. But another piece is that I didn't feel I was that welcome from some people in the football program.

DAVE WAGNER
Dodge City

Wagner's name is familiar to all K-State football fans because it adorns the playing field at Bill Snyder Family Stadium. But he also has a connection to the basketball program. Shortly after graduating from college, he worked on the construction crew that built Jack Hartman's home in Manhattan.

I can remember when Bill Snyder came out here the first time like it was yesterday. We were sitting down and listening to the type of plans he had. He was talking about the value of the young people in the program ... football was important, but it was the other things that would better their lives ... education and that kind of thing.

I remember him saying that we, as fans, owed those kids stuff. He related a couple of stories that he found in talking to his players that they almost enjoyed playing an away game more than the home games because there was more of a crowd. Bill just made the comment that those kids deserved better than that. That the fans needed to buy into the program, get involved, do this and that and so forth.

There was just something about the way he delivered that instead of the "rah rah rah, we were going to go win the Big 8." Here was a guy who was just as low key as we know. It hit a spot with me.

After I won the money (Wagner won a lottery), Steve Miller (athletic director) called me and was congratulating me. I hadn't been taking many calls, but I did take this one.

In K-State's master plan, they had like five different projects they wanted to do. So I listened to the deal and said I would think about it. It all harkens back to Bill's comments about the young guys and building the program and getting people involved.

I thought OK, here's the chance. I could have done a lot of things with the money and so forth, but I said: "I am a K-State fan. We need something to show the players that there are people out there willing to step up."

Building a new press box wasn't going to be the way to do that. There were other things. But a new field would be something that the players would appreciate. They should know that people are out there thinking about them. And maybe it would help other people who are out there and can give and they will buy into the thing and give more.

Dedication day for the field was against Indiana State in 1991. We won, 26-25. I had walked on that field before when the old Wildcat head was on there. They had painted it and done some things like that. It was hard as the street. That dedication day was probably the highlight for our family.

I was born in Ellsworth, Kansas, and grew up in McPherson. Somewhere along the line I just got this affinity for Kansas State. In the group of guys I ran around with in high school, three of us ended up at K-State and three of them ended up at Kansas. I was one of the K-Staters.

Two of my younger brothers both went to KU. But K-State just seemed to fit me and what I felt comfortable with. I graduated from high school in 1960 and was there until 1963 when I enlisted in the Army. I was in for three years and then I came back to K-State and graduated.

I love football, basketball, golf. I liked K-State sports, and I always saw the glass as half-full, not half-empty. It always felt like, yes, the football team was struggling, but they were going to get better. When I came back I was just as much of a die-hard as always. By then Vince was here, so I went through Vince's days.

The year after we beat Oklahoma at home (1969) we went down to Norman the next year and beat them down there. Lew Hafermehl, a good friend of mine from high school and Kansas State, and I were out fishing that day at a farm pond near Manhattan and we had the radio going. When we won that game, somebody who was watching would have seen these two guys out there jumping up and down and hollering and screaming. Maybe Vince is the one who helped convince us that "We Gonna Win" some day.

I didn't have season tickets all the time. We had stayed in Manhattan after I graduated, and both my daughters were born in Manhattan. And they graduated from K-State. We continued going to the games even though I wasn't in school. I remember one time during a losing game that my daughter Jennifer said: "You know dad, why didn't you pick a school that had a winning team?" I said, "Honey, don't worry. They are going to get good. They are going to win. I know it doesn't look very good, but they will."

We moved to Dodge City in the mid-1970s, and at the time the Catbacker organizations were just getting started. I got involved with these guys out here and was helping out the best I could. I was a young working guy with two kids and a wife. So sometimes we didn't have season tickets, but we would get to most-all of the home games. I still had this belief that we were going to win and this thing was going to come around.

I followed basketball, but not quite as feverishly. I remember the old days in Ahearn Field House and what a wonderful time that was for basketball games. But it was easier to get from Dodge City to Manhattan on the football weekends than it was in basketball.

My wife, Lynn, is almost more of a basketball fan than I am. She did not graduate from K-State, but she has become a fan. We have a home in Arizona, and the standing joke is that we wait until after the football season, then after the bowl game, before we go to Arizona because Dave is never ready to go. Now with everything that's going on in basketball it's starting to become a problem for us because she wants to stick around a little longer for basketball. So we try to squeeze in as many as we can before we leave. Thank God they are on TV as much as they are and we have been able to follow them that way. It's great to have two sports that are good.

I have to say it was an absolute delight when the football team began winning. I remember sitting at some of those games, and Jack Vanier and I would look at each other and say: "Is this great or what?" It was payoff time. It's just been a wonderful ride, and I can also relate to my daughter and say: "See, if you wait long enough success will come."

I also have two stepdaughters. They didn't go to K-State, but they are K-State fans. All four of our children are married now and have kids who are also K-State fans. The one in Oklahoma, they are diehard K-Staters. One of our grandsons there, for a long time, he wore his purple to school right there in the heart of OU country. Both of them have K-State backpacks and both wear them to school. And when it's K-State football time, everybody at Nikki's workplace knows it. She also has a Powercat on the car license.

Her husband is from Colorado, and he is a Denver Broncos fan and a CU fan. She followed the Chiefs and K-State. She said she would let the grandkids be Bronco fans, but they had to be K-State fans.

STEVE LEVINE
Manhattan, Kansas

Levine is one of the co-owners of Varney's bookstore in Manhattan, and he has watched as Kansas State fans have demanded more and more school gear to show their purple pride.

One of the neatest things for me is just to see the increased awareness of Kansas State. When I lived in Maryland, no one knew about it. I would go to sports bars in Baltimore and you would have to beg somebody to actually turn the games on. They had like 20 TVs and they were watching the reruns of races at Laurel or somewhere because it had a bigger audience.

My wife's parents live in the area, and when I go back now and I'd have a K-State shirt on, people know where it was from. A kid stopped me and just asked: "How are they going to do this year?" He said he had seen one of the K-State games when he was eight years old and follows them. And I started seeing the little shops that carry all the sports team gear; every now and then there will be a K-State shirt.

Of course, I think everyone should come to Varney's to buy their stuff (laughter).

I have a couple of cool memories; both relate to the store. I was with my dad at one of those big pep rallies at one of the bowl games. He was watching the 20,000 or so people and said: "You know, most of these people have been in our store at one time or another." That was pretty cool.

The other was standing next to Bill Snyder in the store about three years ago when he wrote his book. We had a couple of signings, and it seems like everyone who came through the line had a story: "When this game was happening, I was doing this" or "My grandfather wanted me to say hi to you."

Each one of them wanted him to know how much he had meant to them and how he had touched their lives. One after another, people were saying what he had done for them and what he had done for K-State and how it meant so much to them and their families. That was really a privilege for me to be next to him when all these people came up and wanted to tell him what he meant to them and what K-State meant to them.

I grew up with basketball memories. My family grew up about three blocks from Ahearn Field House. I would walk to games with my father. It was so exciting, watching us beat the Russian National Team right after they had won the Olympics (1972). I remember that moment.

And there was a K-State vs. Missouri game I went to with my brother and we were both in junior high. Missouri was No. 1 and K-State was No. 15. They were announcing the Missouri players, and then when they said: "And now for your ... " You couldn't hear them finish what they were saying. It was the loudest I have ever heard in any stadium. I couldn't hear myself scream. That was the intensity that K-State basketball was. I think it has been matched now with football.

Game days are very fun to watch, especially with the western Kansas fans who are very dedicated. They will travel five, six hours to get to the game. They come to the store and shop and then go support K-State athletics. They are really a unique group of people. In the old days we probably had 20 feet of wall space dedicated to K-State T-shirts and basketballs. Now more than half our first floor is dedicated to K-State athletic apparel and gifts.

After I got out of college, I worked at Prince Georges Community College in Maryland for about six years, then at Eastern Michigan when my wife was getting her Master's at Michigan. She had gone to Penn State and then Michigan and was used to going to games there.

I brought her to a K-State-Nebraska game before we had renovated the stadium. I think there were 38,000 seats. This was before any of the renovations, the parking lot was gravel. She said: "Why do you play in a high school stadium?" That's all changed now, too.

Growing up, we actually went to a lot of Nebraska games in Lincoln because we did a lot of business with the Nebraska Book Company. Ted Varney had actually helped start the company. They would invite my dad up, and of course my brother and I would go up with them to those things that would loosely be termed "games" up in Lincoln.

I always told people if I had my pick between an Oklahoma fan and a Nebraska fan, I would pick an Oklahoma fan. They would both beat us 60-0. But the Nebraska people would be sitting there and say: "Oh, look at our fifth string running up and down the field against you. I am so sorry." The Oklahoma fans, they just wanted to kill you: "C'mon. Let's score again!" At least they thought we were still competition. It was nice to be treated as equals.

It was even nicer when we actually became equals. I remember when I was a kid and Keith Jackson used to do the preview of the Big 8 season that was coming up. Of course we were predicted eighth. He went through all the other schools. He would get to Kansas State University and he would say: "The largest band in the Big 8, over 300..." He talked about our band because there wasn't anything else positive.

One thing I notice about K-State fans, in comparison to like Michigan, is that at Michigan the fans were there enjoying the big games and the spectacle of playing in big games. One game we were playing Nebraska. It was close, and all the fans around were so nervous and on the edge of their seats. I thought, just enjoy it.

They don't really sit back and realize this is fun, win or lose. Here's K-State playing on the national scene. We're competitive. It's not a fluky thing. We're a good team. We're playing Nebraska toe-to-toe; Colorado toe-to-toe. Enjoy it when we're playing KU in basketball because it's a national stage, and we're a good team and it's fun to watch.

Even when the team is good there is a feeling that we are the little dog in the fight. We have to find a way to win and have to use all our tools. We are still K-State and we're not going to get the automatic: "We're KU in basketball" or Nebraska in football.

MICHAEL COOK
Topeka, Kansas

Cook says genetics made him a K-State fan, even though he didn't go to school there. On his mother's side of the family, he is a fourth-generation graduate of Emporia State.

I guess I was a K-State fan before I really understood that there were any other teams. I suspect it's that way for a lot of people. My dad attended K-State and was in the journalism school. I have an uncle who lettered there in 1941. And I did take some classes at K-State after my undergraduate degree.

I can tell you how much being a K-State fan has meant to me. There was a quote from Snyder when he retired – I think he was a little burned out or disillusioned or something. But he said over the years some people had said football was so important to them and they even put it in their family events. He seemed to sound like that was overemphasized.

Christmas for Michael Cook (43) means K-State gear all around.

Photo courtesy of Michelle Cook

I wanted to send him a letter telling him how important it was to my family because it has been a backdrop for our life and it has woven through all the events.

The night I proposed to my wife was during the 1992 season, and Kansas State was playing Iowa State on a really cold night on ESPN. My uncle had gotten me a ticket to go. I went to the game and sat through the first half. It was a close game, but I had really underdressed for it.

My fiancée was having some of the other math grads over to her apartment to watch the game, and I was supposed to go there except I had a ticket. At halftime, I walked to my car and drove to her apartment for the second half. Eric Gallon scored a touchdown, and I proposed ... Yes, she accepted. We had been talking about it, and the rings had come in the previous week.

And there were different games. In 1998 when we beat Nebraska, that was my dad's birthday. It was a great birthday present, especially for a guy like him who had grown up as a K-Stater. But there's a preface to this story.

To take it a step backward, in 1995 we were playing Kansas when both schools were ranked. My dad had been transferred to Indiana, but he came back for this game. Halftime we are ahead by three touchdowns, and I turned to my dad and said: "Isn't this great?" He said: "I have seen us blow bigger leads than this before."

Same thing at the Nebraska game. It's halftime, we're playing pretty well. I went down and talked to him, and he was: "Oh, we're going to lose this game." Even when it was over he was kind of stunned, waiting for the other shoe to drop.

I've never really minded that we would beat the living crap out of nobodies early in the season because I watched a lot of nobodies beating the living crap out of us. I don't think you ever get over that.

We've been season ticket holders for football since 1993, first as student season ticket holders. Once my wife graduated, we got other tickets. I live in Topeka. My parents now live in Abilene, so it makes for a nice gathering. We get together and tailgate before the game together.

My youngest brother went to Purdue. But his whole time he was at Purdue, he was still a K-State fan. The Alamo Bowl was the year before he went to school. He told me that when he goes back to Purdue they still show highlights of that game on the scoreboard. He says every time he watches, it makes him sick.

Sometimes with these things, when you become a fan of something it is a part of your identity. It just sticks there. Even when we weren't going to games, everywhere we went in Kansas, we would always have the radio on 580 (WIBW-

AM). It was the only place you could be guaranteed that K-State games would be on the radio. I remember going and cutting wood in 1979 or 1980 on a Saturday. We were listening to football games and cutting a whole lot of wood out of frustration.

The last couple of years have been like that, too. It didn't look like the players really knew what they were doing like we had been used to. Seeing a team that not only wasn't very good, but also one that seemed to be lost and hopeless. It just kind of sucks the life out of you.

> What does the "N" on Nebraska's football helmets stand for?
>
> "Nowledge."

When Coach Snyder retired, I was talking about who they might hire to replace him. My only comment was that the only guy I ever knew who could win at K-State was Snyder. If anybody can get us back there, he can.

I know from talking with relatives of mine who are farmers that the things Snyder says they can really relate to: "Get a little better every day. It is all hard work, details," etcetera. That kind of stuff just resonates with them. There is a core group of fans who will always stand behind a guy who has integrity.

And I think Frank Martin resonates with people, too. Even though he has a different background, he has that same mentality.

For my dad, football will never be as prominent as basketball because that is the sport he grew up with. If he has to choose between watching a K-State bowl game and an early-tournament game for the basketball team, he is going to go with basketball because that is what he grew up on.

HE WAS A NICE MAN

Michael Cook and his son, Stephen, attended one of those fan days when you get to go down on the field after one of those short practices. My son always liked to go down there and talk to the different players. It didn't matter who as long as they were a K-State player.

Coach Snyder was set up at one of those tables at the 20-yard line, and there was a line that seemed to go on forever. My uncle was waiting to get something signed, and I was standing there talking with him after Stephen had gotten all his signatures.

All of a sudden, I can't find my son anywhere. I didn't panic too much, but there were a lot of people there. So I'm looking around when my uncle taps me on the shoulder and points to the table. My son is standing at the table next to Coach, way up at the front of the line.

It's obvious he cut in front of all of the people in line, so I am looking at their faces as I walk up to get him. But everybody seems to be looking at him and smiling, so I am not too worried. When I get up there I can hear them talking.

Stephen has this little purple blow-up thing that's been deflated, and he's showing it to Coach. Coach asks if he comes to games, then says would it be all right if he signed it. Stephen sort of shrugs his shoulder and says: "Eh, whatever."

Coach has a bunch of purple pens, and he says he will sign it with a special pen and pulls a gray one out of his pocket. Stephen says: "Well, I like the purple ones better."

Coach says: "I know, but if I sign the purple thing with a purple pen you will never be able to see it." So Stephen kind of shrugs his shoulders again, and coach signs it.

Then Coach says "All right, you come back this year and have fun." And Stephen said someday I am going to play here.

About then I get over there, thanked Coach and apologized to the other people in line for him cutting in. So we start to walk away, and I asked Stephen if he had a nice conversation with him.

He said: "Yeah. I don't know who that nice man was ..."

Now the thing is hanging right up on the wall next to the Jordy Nelson picture. But at the time he was just "the nice man at the table."

RICH BAIER
Overland Park, Kansas

Baier didn't have purple in his blood as a youngster. He was a KU basketball fan as he grew up in Spearville, Kansas. But he came to his senses when it came time to enroll in college.

Rich Baier and his family, wife Crysta, daughter Ally and son Joel enjoy a K-State football game.

Photo courtesy of Rich Baier.

I never appreciated the K-State-KU rivalry a whole lot not coming from a K-State family. After I got out of college, I lived in Wichita for several years, and there is a decent balance of fans between K-State and KU. I had a number of friends who went to KU, and the fact that K-State was so dominant in football and KU was so dominant in basketball, there really wasn't a whole lot of reason to get into the rivalry.

But about six years ago we moved to the Kansas City area, and that changed.

There was a feeling of being underappreciated and under recognized if you are a Wildcat fan in Kansas City. I think you feel a little more of a chip on your shoulder. People who didn't even go to KU seem to be KU fans.

And you feel like you are sort of pushed into a corner as a K-State fan. I make it a point to wear my purple as often as I can just so it's seen out there. It doesn't mean anything in the grand scheme of things. But it's just a little bit of rebel in me, I guess, that I want people to know I am not going to be pushed into a corner and made to feel less of a fan just because I am a K-State fan in Kansas City.

My wife went to Emporia State. The first few years we were married, she thought that chip I had about the KU-K-State thing was stupid. Now, after having lived in Kansas City for a few years, she says: "Yeah, now I can see it."

But all the Kansas State fans seem to bond, something as simple as driving down the road and you see a car pass by you with a Powercat on the license plate. You honk, you wave, you say "Go 'Cats." I probably am not real consistent with your average K-Stater in what I believe in, but that's always something you can bond with.

I grew up in rural southwest Kansas in a graduating class of 29 or 30. But I knew I wanted to go to a bigger school and experience something different. For a lot of kids in western Kansas, that seems to be a school like K-State. It is a nice balance between wanting to get out and experience something bigger and not having to go to New York or L.A.

When I was in high school, football was kind of a joke for both schools (KU and K-State), and you couldn't be much of a fan for either school. And much as I am kind of ashamed to admit it, I guess I would have had to call myself a KU basketball fan growing up. I came to my senses eventually.

It was definitely football that got me excited about Kansas State when they started to turn things around. I think it was 1993, Chad May's first year when they got to a bowl game for the first time. Everything was new and exciting, and that is when I got the bug. It was also before we got too spoiled and expectations were too high.

I was a season ticket holder my sophomore, junior, and senior seasons and I have been ever since. I have always been a big football fan, played football in high school. So it didn't take much to get me excited about football.

Right now it isn't exactly a great time to be a K-State fan with all the mess that's going on. It seems like something that should have happened at Missouri instead of K-State. It's pretty embarrassing, and to some extent the Wefald legacy has been damaged, though I don't feel sorry for him.

But there seems to be an optimism that there is a new sheriff in town, a new leadership team. While they are not starting with a clean slate, they can say: "Hey, we were not a part of that mess. We're going to clean it up and make things better going forward."

I wasn't all that pumped at first when Bill Snyder took over as football coach again. I thought it was kind of an odd choice. But you see the sort of renewed energy and enthusiasm that he has, and it seems like he is making waves on the recruiting trail.

At least we will see a team that is prepared and disciplined and works hard and doesn't quit until the end. We haven't been seeing that, especially the last year. Prince was all style and no substance. He fooled a lot of people with perceptions and good press conferences and good quotes. There was a false sense of confidence in the way things were going. That was exposed pretty quickly.

As far as Frank Martin goes, he looks like somebody who was in one of those mafia movies. But he has sort of a Midwest chip on his shoulder, sort of a K-State thing. He always plays that underdog card. Every once in a while he says something that sort of makes you cringe but I love that guy. In an odd way he seems to resonate with people and they seem to be getting more and more comfortable with it every day.

I have a lot of family out in western Kansas, and I was back there over Memorial Day for an extended family get together. I don't have a single relative who went to KU, but I go out there and see all my relatives are wearing KU T-shirts and have KU plates on their car.

A number of my family members are involved in agriculture out in western Kansas. I didn't say anything, but I was thinking to myself whether they had any idea what most KU students think of anyone west of Topeka.

DENNIS BOONE
Kansas City

Boone didn't begin detesting the Jayhawks until his first trip to Memorial Stadium in Lawrence for a K-State-KU game. It became a blood feud when his younger brother, Joe Boone, walked on and earned a starting spot on the K-State defense in 1989.

There was nothing about the program that had really drawn me in as a fan. I was sort of neutral even on KU until that first year in Lawrence. I was in the stands and heard some of the things they were saying about K-State. I thought: "Geez, they hate us! Why?"

I had gone to K-State about 10 years earlier. I had been working at *The Kansas City Star* out of high school and Cruise Palmer, one of the editors, kept urging me to go to college. I remember going with a friend to the Big 8 basketball title game in Kansas City in 1976. It was K-State and Missouri.

We had gone to Crown Center before the game, and he had an adult beverage. I had just turned 21, so I probably did, too. We listened to a little jazz, and I told him that whoever wins this game, it is a sign from God, and that is where I am going to journalism school.

In the first half, Missouri is up by 15 or something, and I am thinking "Uh-oh, out of state tuition." But K-State cut it to 10 at halftime, then won it in overtime.

I became a much bigger fan when it became a blood connection to the team. When (Jim) Dickey was coaching, I was a student correspondent. Mom and Dad brought Joe and my other little brother – the KU idiot – down to the game when they were 9 and 13. I had Joe with me when I walked into Dickey's office the day after the game.

Missouri had beaten them the day before, but I can remember Joe looking out over that field. Dickey said: "Son, you want to play football here some day?" Joe said "Yes sir."

I always thought back to that first look out on the field when he was playing there.

He would have gone to Lawrence, but they wouldn't give him a scholarship and wouldn't entertain the idea of him possibly earning one. So he went to Coffeyville for a year, redshirted and then moved up to Manhattan when Snyder got hired. I saw every one of those games the first three years, home and away – including the stompings in Boulder and at Washington.

Another incident that soured me on Kansas is when I was an intern out in Olathe. I had to interview some judge for a story. We were sitting in his office.

He said: "You just get out of school?"

"Yes sir"

"Where'd you go to school?"

"K-State."

"You know how to find Manhattan?"

"Yes sir, I have been there a number of times."

"No, you go west until you smell it and north until you step in it."

I'm thinking, Dude, I just met you. Why do you do that?

I also have a favorite Missouri story from when my brother was playing. Joe's senior year, they were playing in the rain. K-State won that day, 32-0. MU had fumbled 11 times and lost six or something like that. And by the fourth quarter this thing is sealed. All you want to do is get off the field.

I look down, and Joe was still playing. He's lining up over center, and all of a sudden his head snaps up. There's some trash talk coming at him, and Joe is yakking back at the center. There is another response and another. I've always wondered what those guys actually say to each other, and I'm thinking I have an opportunity to find out. So after the game I ask him. Now keep in mind it's 32-0.

He said the guy came up on the ball and said: "Coming at you, K-State."

Joe said: "Bring it."

Then the guy said: "Hey, don't you laugh at me. We ain't no Western Illinois."

Joe said: "You're right. They scored on us."

The thing I always took away from being a fan, especially after I got involved when Joe started playing there, was what I learned from a distance from Snyder about the power of incremental improvement. It's not just a football thing. It will work the same way for a business, or a marriage. Start working on the little things that can be successful, and things will turn around.

Bill has a vision, and he understood detail. If you are better just one little tick in each of those 11 games in the first year and then each of the 11 games in the next year and the next year, you reach a point where there aren't that many ticks between 9-2-1 and 11-0 and literally could come down to a fumble at a critical time.

Think about how narrow the margin between real, outstanding success and mediocrity is. If (Jeron) Mastrud doesn't drop that pass on the 5 in Boulder, the field goal wins them the game. Then they're probably going to a bowl game, and they have another month of practice to get better. And Ron Prince probably doesn't get fired.

Snyder always understood that every play could make or break your season. I think he approached his instruction that way. For some reason when I saw Prince's teams play it was: "Yeah, they got 30 on that play, but they ain't getting 30 on the next one." You don't need many 30-yard bursts to get into the end zone.

I'm glad Snyder came back because I think he will establish something this time that will set a standard for the interviews for his successor. I hope they are going to want to know in much greater detail how you would plan out a program that in business you would call a continuous improvement cycle. In some ways it might be better for Bill. He had lost control of some things. It's not like Prince came in and wrecked a stellar program. There had been two really mediocre years.

Sure, it's harder to be a fan right now, just as it was hard for KU who wanted to see a winning football program in the 1990s to have to look across the state and think: "Those bastards."

It's hard for K-Staters now, especially for me. I was on campus the night K-State beat the Russian National Team in basketball. I think they were the only college team ever to do that, and it was a big honking deal. I was just crazy about basketball then. It was just heartbreak after Lon (Kruger) left and wrecked everything there. We really thought in 1988 that there were going to be many great things ahead, even though fate came in and crapped on our heads in Auburn Hills.

Joe and I still get together for big games and go out to his house and watch them. Usually there is some beer involved, and if it turns out right, we'll be out peeing on Paul's Jayhawk rock on his front porch in the middle of the night.

BRIAN GATES
Beloit, Kansas

Gates became a Wildcats fan before he even knew there were other teams – good parenting skills, of course. Now he's not only a fan, he's the go-to guy for all things recruiting around Kansas State basketball and football for Powercat Illustrated.

Growing up in our house, there wasn't much chance of being anything but a K-State fan. Mom and Dad both went to K-State. We had season tickets for football going back to before they got good – the old family plan season tickets area. We didn't go to every game, but that's just kind of what we did. We went to basketball games in Ahearn. That's what I was exposed to so that's why I became a fan.

I did go to Kansas State. There was never any question about that. That was decided early – by me and everyone else.

I am not quite as publicly vocal about being a K-State fan now that I have been working for *Powercat Illustrated*. I was never afraid to place the wager with the secretary at school who was a KU fan or other students who were KU fans. I am pretty die-hard all the way through and never really had much love for the Jayhawks.

It has been a real part of my family's life. My parking pass is next to my Mom and Dad's, and my sister's is on the other side. My kids wear their basketball jerseys and football jerseys all the time. They are as purple as I am – or they will be eventually.

Snyder won one game my senior year in high school, then I was there for the five-win season, then seven, then complaining we weren't getting to a bowl game. I'll never forget the Copper Bowl we went to. It's no National Championship, but it is an experience I will never forget. I don't know what the number has grown to now, but there were 15,000 or whatever it was K-State fans in the stadium. The 52-17 final score. The punt return by Andre Coleman ... Chad May and Kevin Lockett and all those things.

There just wasn't any better feeling than that at the time. That's why when everyone is discussing the bowls and the playoff situation ... I am not sure I want a playoff if it means the bowl situation will change. I don't want them to disappear. That experience would never have happened, and it's something I will never forget. I would hate for fans to not have that opportunity.

And I've loved basketball, as well. I faintly remember going to games in Ahearn. When I got to school, Coach Altman was there. This resurgence with Hugs (Bob Huggins) and Coach Martin now, this is just great. If I had to pick one, I would probably go to a basketball game if you made me have to pick. But the football is nice, and I am happy that Coach Snyder is back.

The recruiting thing (his expertise in the subject) happened just with me being a fan with my roommate and following it in school. We were really following the recruitment of J.R. Rider from Allen County, and I don't know how many of those recruiting newsletters we subscribed to. Those are the ones that are already out of date by the time they get to you because of the printing and mailing time. The Internet has really changed that.

> What does the "O" on Oklahoma's football helmets stand for?
>
> "Onor."

In football, there wasn't any coverage then. That was 1989 and 1990. It was even tough to find out who K-State had signed. There was a press release that came out. I don't know if the *Collegian* (the K-State campus newspaper) even had anything about it. But you sure didn't know anything about these kids six months ahead of time or a year. But the basketball, we knew everything about the basketball recruits that were being recruited.

1997 is probably the first year I really followed the football recruiting. I kept bothering Tim (Fitzgerald, editor of *Powercat Illustrated*) enough that he said: "Call them yourself, and you can write it up for me." That was the (Michael) Bishop class. Boy, what a class that was with so many of them panning out. I think there were 27 in the class with 13 or 14 juco guys. There were a really good number of performers at a high level. Not just starters, they were All-Conference and All-America in that group.

Because of the recruiting thing, I feel like I know those guys a little more than the average fan because I have talked to them for a year. In the case of basketball players, sometimes it is two years. But when I am actually at an event, I try not to analyze any of their plays. So I don't think that has affected me as a fan.

But it sure has affected my life. During the football season on Sundays we make a lot of calls when kids have been to campuses and visited. Basketball is kind of a year-round deal. I have always told Tim I would do it as long as I continued enjoying it, then I would stop because I didn't want it to become a job. But it's a labor of love and it's fun to do right now.

I don't know if I can single out any one thing that has been the most memorable experience. The 1998 Big 12 championship game was just a killer. I was here (in Beloit, Kansas). The K-State game was on the TV in the living room, and UCLA (vs. Miami) was in the kitchen. When UCLA lost there was a celebration. K-State was up whatever it was at the time, and you just knew K-State was going to finish this off and be playing for the National Championship. It just fell apart.

The 2003 Big 12 Championship. That's an evening we will never forget. I wasn't there for that game, either. For being a great fan, I never go to these games, do I? But I remember thinking when it was 7-7 in that game and I told the three or four guys watching with me, here comes the pump-fake bomb to James Terry like they did in Nebraska. Sure enough they did that play.

I certainly didn't have any inside knowledge, and Coach Snyder wasn't calling me to ask anything (laughter). But that was the play that put K-State ahead and they went on from there. Sproles ... that was a performance for all time.

In basketball my favorite things were getting to the games early enough that you could get to the front row all the time. Coach Altman knew your name. And Pete Hermann, an assistant under Coach Altman, would come over and sit down and talk for 15-20 minutes. So just getting to know the people.

And when I was a freshman, watching the goal posts come down my first game as a student. That was a blast. It was in 1990. I don't even remember who it was, but it was a nobody. That much I am certain of. Why the goal posts would come down for Western Illinois, I don't know. But it was only the second time in 12 games that Coach Snyder had won a game.

Probably the other game was the Oklahoma game in 1993 (a 21-7 win). I know it wasn't a huge victory scorewise, but I remember that was kind of a "Hey America, K-State is for real!"

BRENDAN FORREST
Olathe, Kansas

Forrest didn't really follow sports in high school, but he was infected with the purple virus shortly after arriving at Kansas State in the late 1980s and was quickly immersed in all things Wildcat. His daughter's softball team uniform is purple, for the Purple Panthers, and he's not sure the Jayhawk parents on the team realize how he came to the color purple.

Neither of my parents was interested in sports and didn't pay attention to that stuff, and as a byproduct of that I didn't, either. In fact, if you had asked me who won the national championships in 1988, I wouldn't have been able to tell you. It was just one of those things I didn't pick up on or pay attention to.

I was in one of the first groups of people when Kansas State started making a pretty strong push in Kansas high schools to get kids to go there after Jon Wefald became president. I didn't know a whole lot about Kansas State, but the fact that it was about two hours away from Kansas City was a pretty big factor. It got me a little distance away from my parents, and I didn't have to worry about them just dropping in on me.

I had visited Emporia. I looked at KU. I looked at Baker. When we went up to K-State and visited they were really friendly and recruited me heavily. The person who visited our high school was the same person we had all the way through the process. We knew her by her first name and she knew us by sight. I can say this with a little tongue-in-cheek now, but when KU came and visited our high school they just sort of tossed some brochures out and said: "Hey, we're KU and here we are." That was one of the big differences at that time for me.

When I got up there, I joined a fraternity. The guys in the fraternity were pretty much into it and went to all the games. I went to all the basketball games and all the football games. After I graduated in 1995, some of the guys I had graduated with, we ended up getting season tickets. It was kind of the heyday of the football team. It was easy to get pulled into it.

Basketball? When I first got up there Dana Altman was still their coach. I hadn't followed any of that very closely, so I didn't have any real perception of what the basketball program was. I hadn't realized K-State had gotten into the

Elite Eight in 1988 and played KU and that they had beaten them a couple of times during the season. For me Dana Altman was doing a pretty good job.

He had them in and out of the Top 25. He had beaten Top 25 schools. We ran Oklahoma out of the gym one game. Dana had beaten KU in one of the Big 8 tournaments (1993) … Anthony Beane and Aaron Collier and Deryl Cunningham and Askia Jones … to me those guys were pretty good and it was a good basketball team. They weren't going to win the National Championship, but it was a good enough basketball team for me.

So it was kind of surprising to me that people were disappointed in the basketball team until I actually was figuring out what the history was. Then I realized how good they had actually been and what the expectations were. But I still think people over-reacted to his tenure and we paid the price for that mistake for more than 10 years.

I don't get to as many games now. My Saturdays started getting fuller when my son got to be about 6 or 7 years old and was playing sports. I just didn't maintain the season tickets any more. I made it up for Snyder's last game against Missouri. Every season since I have tried to take my son up for a game, and we try to go to one of the basketball games just so he gets a feel for it and I get a little taste for going back. I did go up last year for the Oklahoma game, and the whole thing just didn't have the vibe it did a few years back.

One thing, I don't really run into a whole lot of bandwagon K-State fans. You are either a K-State fan or not. It's not like KU. I have never run into anybody who has gone to K-State or their parents had gone to K-State and they had a direct tie to the university who is a bandwagon fan. I would have to say that K-State fans are kind of pessimistic. We always think we are going to lose the game or the worst possible thing is going to happen.

In Kansas City sometimes I get ticked off because it seems like (Jason) Whitlock and (Joe) Posnanski take a little extra joy in taking shots at K-State – and Jack Harry whenever he gets a chance. Kevin Kietzman, who I know is a dedicated K-State guy, seems like he is the one guy who actually takes pains to try and be fair and balanced and not be a homer. So that gets frustrating and leads to a little pessimism and a chip on the shoulder.

But like I said, I have never run into anybody who is a K-State fan who is a bandwagon fan. You are either a K-State fan or you are not. It does feel a lot like a community. When I see a car with a Wildcat license plate on it, I have a pretty good feeling that guy or girl went to K-State and they are watching the games and suffering every time we lose and celebrating when we have a good win.

KEVIN KIETZMAN
Kansas City sports talk show host

The K-State football team went to its first bowl game in Kietzman's freshman year in college, but the bug didn't really bite him until he could begin sharing the experience with his children.

My very best memories aren't of a single game but the whole Bill Snyder football era in the stands. Because of the job I had, I was finally working Monday through Friday and no weekends. I could go up there on Saturdays. I had my boys with me. I went to all those games with my kids. They were raised on it. They had something really to grasp on to, and it became a destination for them.

They could think: I want to grow up and I want to go to college. It got them to thinking as children that my school doesn't end when I am 18. I would walk them down to the student section. That whole atmosphere in the Snyder era was just electric. There were just some unbelievable moments.

My older brother was the first from our family to go to college. He is seven years older than me. My parents both were from right near Manhattan. My mom was from Paxico, Kansas, and my dad was from Alma, Kansas. But the concept of colleges or college athletics was kind of foreign to me growing up as a kid because it wasn't something that was talked about in our home.

When I went to college (1982-86) it was like the football team didn't exist. You didn't tell anybody there was a football team at K-State. No, I was up there to see Rolando Blackman and Eddie Nealy play. I was an avid fan, but mostly basketball.

We went to most of the football games and had a great time. But it was mostly social. I think at the time they had a policy that coolers were legal. I saw a guy come into the game in a wheelchair with a keg underneath his seat. It was cold and everything, so he had blankets on the wheelchair. But he pulled it off.

The only game we didn't go to was the Nebraska game. We sold our tickets to Nebraska fans. We knew it would be a terrible game, and our season tickets were like a meal ticket. They punched the number of the game when you went through the gate.

We quickly learned that if you sold that to a Nebraska fan at the stadium, they would give you more than the whole season ticket was worth, and they would mail it back to you.

The basketball was really good right after I left. Kruger was coming in. We had the Elite Eight year. The loss to Kansas was just devastating. If you look at the histories of the two programs, they were pretty similar up to that moment with K-State maybe being a little better. But since then Kansas has gotten better and better and better. K-State had gone way downhill until just recently.

That game against KU in the Elite Eight and the Texas A&M football game were the two lowest moments ever. We were pretty sure we had the better basketball team, and we had just beaten Kansas a couple of weeks earlier. Everyone thought this was great. We get to go to the Final Four, and we get to beat Kansas to do it.

The Texas A&M game. We were dead sure we were in. That day we started out thinking we would win by 30 and we were still not in because we didn't control it. Then everything went right. We have the best team in the country and we're winning and this is going to be great. I reserved 13 tickets on Southwest Airlines at halftime. We booked all those flights.

We went from the greatest time in our lives to ... you would have thought we had been to a funeral. The devastation after that was just awful. We went to get something to eat after the game, and we just sat there. We didn't even talk. I think everyone was just mortified.

Boy, if we just had that KU game back in 1988. If we could just have that football game against A&M ...

If we just had one of these events, then we wouldn't have this chip on our shoulder. We could always play this one card on anybody who tried to give us a hard time about being a K-State fan. We would always have this one card. But we just don't have that card.

The horribleness – if there is even such a word – was to go from the euphoria of being in to the devastation. We finally felt like what it was to be in. We had wanted that all year and it was never there. We had wanted that our whole lives and never experienced it. We were dead sure, and convinced we were in. You have the best running quarterback we have seen in our life and he just has to hang on to the ball.

STEVEN WATKINS
Topeka, Kansas

Watkins' father suffered a heart attack while attending a game at Ahearn Field House. He recovered, and it became part of the lore connecting the Watkins family to Kansas State athletics. Although she would never take credit for it, his daughter, Caroline, was a dancer in the Classy Cats and may well have set the tone for the 2003 Big 12 championship game against Oklahoma – though Watkins and his wife didn't even see the incident.

For some reason we had fabulous seats for that championship game, but we got caught up in traffic and didn't get to the game before it started. Before the game, the Classy Cats were on the field with the band in the pregame, and either OU was coming on or going off the field and started intentionally bumping into the band members and the Classy Cats. There was sort of a brouhaha because somebody was supposed to get out of the way.

I don't know all the facts about it, but the Classy Cats refused to move. There was this little redhead who was standing up against these OU guys who were being sort of intimidating. Sort of a Tianamen Square event.

I was mad because we were late. We had just gotten out of the car in the parking lot, and the moment we got out we could hear the roar of the crowd from the OU fans. Somehow we were aware that before we had even gotten to the game, OU had scored. There were some OU fans arriving late and whooping it up, and we were thinking why are we even going to this game.

But it turned into just a joyful night. It was just crazy. Darren Sproles just went nuts, and what a joyful night it was for the likes of us. It was wonderful.

It was just the opposite in 1998. It was one of the worst experiences of our lives, honestly, when we lost to Texas A&M. It was just horrible. I think it was in the post-game interview that Bill Snyder said something to the effect that it felt like somebody had died.

The Watkins make it a family affair with Steven (left), Diane, Steve Jr., Caroline and Barbara. Steve Jr. a graduate of West Point, was visiting home from Iraq.
Photo courtesy Steven Watkins family

He was roundly criticized for that by everyone in the media, and I remember thinking at the time: "Why? Have you ever wanted something so badly in your life and it failed?" Everybody felt like somebody died. I was so angry that people criticized him for that comment. That's how we all felt. And it made us all feel even worse because we sense how deeply he felt about that.

I sort of grew up in a K-State household. My dad went to K-State right after the war. He slept on the floor of Nichols Gym a few nights before he could find a place to stay. My mom went there. I knew I wanted to go to KU Med school, and my best friend in high school went to KU. So I strongly considered going to KU. I honestly don't remember what made my final decision other than just the loyalty I had for K-State. It was a better fit for me personality-wise and my family history.

I had become entranced by the radio broadcasts of Kansas State sports. It would have been the late 1950s when I began remembering that stuff. I don't know if Dev Nelson went back that far. But I was just hypnotized by what I perceived as the glamour of K-State sports, mostly basketball games with Jack Parr and Willie Murrell. I don't remember much about football, probably for good reason.

Once I got to K-State I absolutely loved it. I met my wife there, and we have been married for 37 years. Two of our three children went there. My daughter, Diane, went there and roomed with Kerri Korsak, the daughter of my wife's college roommate. My son went to West Point. My second daughter, Caroline, became a Classy Cat and was captain of the Classy Cats her senior year.

After my wife and I graduated, we left the state. I was in the Air Force before coming back to Topeka in 1982. And really, all those years, we were not in touch with K-State sports; we just shelved it for all those years. In 1982, we started going to K-State football games again. We would take the kids. My son would have been 7 or 8, and he would spend the whole game running around the stadium up and down the stairs, wherever he wanted to go. Having young children, we didn't want to get there too early, so we would walk up at the last minute, get tickets and sit wherever we wanted.

In 1982 it was the bowl year, as lame as it was. And we went to the Independence Bowl. But it was a pretty miserable experience from start to finish. Several families from Emporia went together in an RV. The thing broke down twice on the way down there. It was freezing cold, and nobody brought a raincoat. I wore a trash bag over myself during the game, and some fan from the other team said I looked like a used condom – which is not very polite, but part of our lore now.

We kept going to the games, and obviously it became more fun. We began tailgating with the Korsak family. My wife is sort of a history buff, and when tailgating really began to take off on the west side of the stadium, with all the banners and everything, she would say it reminded her of a medieval or renaissance festival. There were banners and people wearing costumes with meat cooking and music going. Since she said that we have always thought about that in terms of tailgating.

We didn't really do much with basketball until the kids got quite a bit older. We have season tickets now and have for several years. It wasn't until Caroline was there that we started going to a lot of basketball games. We watched her dance for four years and have kept them going even after that.

There is a good thing and a bad thing about K-State fans. The good thing to me is that K-Staters, on the average, represent the Midwest work ethic, the Midwest attitude. They are not haughty. They don't have a sense of entitlement. I just love that K-State atmosphere and the K-State fans.

They are very loyal and they follow their football team out of state.

The bad thing is that they are defensive because they have had the short end of the stick on the sports field to some extent and because of who they are and where they come from, I think they overreact to negative things in the press and so on – including me. I don't think it's bad to have a chip on your shoulder. I played a lot of sports, and I had that same attitude when I played sports. I had that chip on my shoulder, and it does help some things.

MAX JANTZ
Montezuma, Kansas

Jantz's daughter, Heather, and son, Aaron, got him hooked on attending K-State football games in the mid 1990s.

One of my favorite memories was going down to watch our team play at Texas. It was 2007. Ian Campbell was playing for us. His dad is a friend of mine, and he was named Defensive Player of the Week in the Big 12 that week. He just had a great game, and we beat Texas.

But I remember walking in to that game, and it is all Texas fans all around with that orange color. There are a few purple people walking in. An older gentleman came up to us. He was real nice, and he looked at us and started visiting.

He said: "We'll find out what kind of team we have next week."

I asked who they were playing next week, and he said it was the OU-Texas game the week after us. They were looking completely past Kansas State. I thought to myself, you guys had better deal with us first.

He was a real nice guy and all excited about going in to the game. Anyway, we go in there, and it was in the third quarter or so. We have a friend from down there we buy supplies for, and we're sitting in seats he got for us right on the 50-yard line about 28 rows up. We're sitting right there in the middle of all these Texas people, and they're all pretty subdued by this time. But one of them turned around and looked at us and said: "What's you guy's record?"

They just absolutely didn't know K-State existed, and we had beaten them three out of four times or something like that. A lot of those fans left before the game was over. I can say this about Texas: when we were down there and beat them, they would be complimentary to us. But as far as they were concerned about their team, they just played awful.

My daughter, Heather, went to K-State starting her junior year. She started out at Barton County Community College and went two years there. Then she transferred to KU for one semester, and it just wasn't her type of place. Then she went to Fort Hays State and then landed up at K-State and just loved it and wished she had gone there the whole time. My son, Aaron, went all four years. It would have been around 1996 before I became a real K-State fan. That's when we started attending most of the games.

Oh, you know, we would take sports trips when the kids were in high school, and we usually went to a K-State football or basketball game. This is K-State country out here where we live. But we weren't "regulars" until my daughter went up there.

We did some basketball, and here a couple of years ago I did get season tickets for basketball – Frank's first year. It's kind of tough for me to make it up for basketball games when they play them during the week.

For the football games we share a suite with another family, and I think we have about 14 tickets in our half of the suite. The kids are back here working in the business, and we make it a family deal. They usually leave Dad four tickets.

We just enjoy the atmosphere, and it gives us a day off, a day to relax and go enjoy yourself. It's just good fun to follow along and watch the team.

RICK KUEKER
Belleville, Kansas

Kueker attended Kansas State during some of basketball's glory years in the 1970s, then went to medical school at the University of Kansas Medical Center. After a side trip for his residency in Boise, Idaho, Keuker came back to Kansas to practice medicine and Kansas State athletics have been his family's entertainment – and touchstone.

I used to think I could hear 580 (WIBW-AM) in Boise, Idaho, late at night. A few times I literally stood out on a corner and thought I could pick up bits and pieces of the games. One night I was standing out there on the curb listening to what I thought was the game and my dad would call my wife and tell me how the game had ended 15 minutes before.

When I was in school, my roommates would always camp out and stand in line; for the Missouri and Kansas games, they would camp out for days. They would always get us good seats and get us in line for when that big garage door would open up and the mass would go through that thing.

My wife, who is pretty small and petite, used to say that from the time that crowd started moving toward those doors, her feet would not touch the ground until she was on the court. The mob would just carry her along. It was a miracle that people weren't killed. It was not uncommon when that first mass of students would hit that first row of bleachers, the impact of the first wave would break one or two of them. They would have to come out and repair them before the game.

When I was in medical school, that was 1976-79 in Kansas City, Jack Hartman had it going pretty good. We made it over to Manhattan some. Then I was in my residency in Boise, Idaho, when Rolando (Blackman) made that shot and made the cover of *Sports Illustrated.* Those years were kind of a blur because I was on-call most of the time and working on not too much sleep. But we did get to go to Salt Lake City for the next weekend.

Rick Kueker, daughter Richelle and wife, Susan, at a Kansas State basketball game.
Photo courtesy of Rick Kueker family

For us the highlight was probably the 1988 team. Lon and Dana, Mitch Richmond, Steve Henson. That team was good, and the Big 8 was so good that year. Making it to the Midwestern Regional Finals. I remember waking up the morning of the game, and one of the Detroit papers had the headline "Kansas Wildcats play the Kansas State Jayhawks" ...

We had taken our kids to the Big 8 tournament, then to South Bend for the first round and then to Detroit. We arranged for the five kids to get all their work done and get out of school. It was really nice that the principal took the approach it was a great opportunity for them to go and enjoy it and have fun rather than "OK, you better not get sick another day this year!" type thing.

Ralph Kueker and his great granddaughter Cadence represent four generations of K-State fans in the Kueker family.

Photos courtesy of Rick Kueker family

None of them was struggling. So we would go, my folks would go. There was quite a family of us. That year, I don't remember if it was in South Bend or in Detroit, we had a room by Freddy McCoy. There were these pizza boxes out in the hallway all the time, and the kids couldn't figure out where they were coming from until we realized he was in a room right by us.

A couple of years ago, we were flying somewhere and my youngest and middle son were at the airport talking to a guy. It was Chauncey Billups. They were talking and laughing, and when we got on the plane they tell me that he still thinks about the Big 8 tournament as being one of his all-time favorite basketball tournaments.

And even though I love basketball, you would have to say the Big 12 championship win over Oklahoma was a highlight. Matt had a basketball game here in Concordia on Friday night and had a game Saturday afternoon in Silver Lake. Some of the family didn't think we could make the game. By the time we got to I-70 outside Arrowhead, I think

K-State was already down 7-0. We walked into the stadium right behind the OU section, and we got kind of blasted. But from then on it was all-K-State.

People don't realize how big that win was. Everybody was talking about them (OU) being the best team ever. They kind of disappeared. And they still played for the National Championship.

Another big game was the year we beat KU in Lawrence when they were No. 1 (1993-94). Dana had Anthony Beane hold the ball for 45 seconds or so and he drove down the lane for the win. To this day, I don't think Roy Williams has ever let anybody stand there and hold the ball like that again. He always goes out and makes him get rid of the ball.

And we also got the scare of our lives with the basketball team the year before. We were at the NCAA Regional in Orlando, and were at one of the parks. We had two big groups of K-State fans. The team was in one and we were in the other with Mitch Holthus and our wives and families. We weren't paying enough attention and all of a sudden we realized we had four kids instead of five. We couldn't find Matt anywhere.

So I am jogging around the park for an hour. My mom and dad sat at the entrance making sure nobody got out of there with him. Everybody in the group was looking. Lo-and-behold, I see Vincent Jackson and Anthony Beane. Matt has been riding rides with them. I don't know how they got him on the rides because he was probably only 7 at the time. He was riding with the players, unconcerned.

CHAPTER 4
Living with the Enemy

As the seconds ticked down that January night in 2008, Kansas State fans were poised for the largest celebration in Bramlage Coliseum history. The Wildcats were closing in on their first-ever home win over the Kansas Jayhawks since they began playing basketball away from Ahearn Field House in 1988.

Fans who were at the game report getting chills as they realized the long drought against the arch-rivals was about to end.

Three freshmen – Michael Beasley with 25 points, Bill Walker with 22, and Jacob Pullen with 20 – were the architects as the 22nd-ranked Wildcats upset the No. 2-ranked Jayhawks, 84-75.

Pandemonium followed. Students and other fans rushed to the floor. Older fans, unwilling to risk bodily injury, grinned from ear to ear. Beasley stood on a table alongside the court celebrating.

The next day, at water coolers all across Kansas, Wildcat fans rejoiced as they do with every victory over the University of Kansas. In their world there is no larger rivalry than the one with the Jayhawks.

Kansas State football fans cherished the 11 straight wins over the Jayhawks from 1993-2004.

Basketball fans love the early years of the Big 8 Conference with five league championships in the first six years. The highlight of the Jim Wooldridge years – and there were not a lot of highlights – was the win over Kansas in Allen Fieldhouse.

The Sunflower Showdown is front-page news in Kansas every year. The only place where it doesn't reign supreme is along the state line where the Kansas-Missouri Border War rivalry holds sway as the most important.

But for Kansas State fans – and for all of Kansas west of Lawrence – the in-state game for bragging rights is the most important of the year.

There are "mixed" marriages with K-State fans paired up with fans of other schools. There are K-State fans attending other schools in the Big 12.

There is a small, but enthusiastic cadre of fans who live in the shadow of Allen Fieldhouse in Lawrence or just down the block from KU's Memorial Stadium. License plates with "KSU Wildcats" adorn their cars. Powercats appear in the middle of the official state license plate.

They personify "living with the enemy."

✳ ✳ ✳

LORA GILLILAND-SCHNEIDER
Lawrence, Kansas

Gilliland-Schneider has been a rebel as long as she can remember, going against the grain as early as her selection of college: Kansas State, of course.

When I moved to Lawrence, the moving company gave us a truck that had Powercats all over it. One of my neighbors came and saw the truck and he started to shake his head like "there goes the neighborhood." But we all became fast friends, and it is fun. You always have that bet on whose team is going to win.

> **Every once in a while I get waved at with one finger, but I just assume they are busy and didn't have time to put up the other four.**

I drive a white car with K-State stuff on it, and my license plate reads KSU Cat. We count the Powercats daily. It's something my kids and I do. My kids are always: "Look, there's a Wildcat. There's a Wildcat."

Every once in a while I get waved at with one finger, but I just assume they are busy and didn't have time to put up the other four.

Lora, Robin Spencer and football coach Bill Snyder at a Lawrence Catbacker function in 2008.

Photo courtesy of Lora Gilliland-Schneider

Both of my parents were Fort Hays people. My older sister went to Bethany. I've just always been one to go against the grain, and I had friends who liked KU. I said forget you, I like K-State. That's pretty much how it went.

When I went to college in 1987, it was kind of hard for me. All my friends were going to Fort Hays. But K-State is where I always wanted to go. It wasn't even a question once I got to a certain age.

I wanted to do something in radio and television journalism. K-State had a very good school. I went up for my visit and got a warm, fuzzy feeling about the place and said "That's where I am going."

It was like a family. Former basketball player Mitch Richmond, who was in the same dorm I was in, said the same thing. He always said: "They made me feel like this is the place I am supposed to be."

Lora and her son Jackson at the K-State–Texas game.

Photo courtesy of Lora Gilliland-Schneider

I liked that we had a good basketball team. Football was just a place to go hang out and get rowdy with your friends. Back in the day, the fall of 1987, when you told your friends that you would see them at the game, you actually meant you would *see* them. You could look at them across the empty stadium. You will hear people say this a million times: if I had spare football tickets and put two on my windshield wipers, I would come back and find four more with them.

I lived on the same dorm floor as most of the girls on the basketball team. I knew Tony Massop and Mitch and some of those guys. It was fun to go and root for people I actually knew. To me it was funny when people would say: "Oh wow, Mitch Richmond is awesome." I would say: "Yeah, I just talked to him this morning."

Elyse Funk was a point guard for the women's team. I knew some guys who thought she was wonderful, she was so pretty. I was thinking: "Oh, that's just Elyse." That is what I like about college sports. They were just students and kids like I was.

There were some humiliating moments. I remember the football players from Austin Peay break dancing on the Wildcat in the middle of the field after they beat us, those types of moments. But as humiliating as it was, you went home, you rubbed a little dirt on your wound and got up the next day and went on about it. It wasn't something we sat around and cried about.

The nice thing about us getting a winning team was finally seeing the good people get a little recognition, the accolades they deserved. And finally people couldn't say your school sucks because you don't have a good football team. While I knew my school's football team wasn't great, it was still a great school. But for some reason it took that for people to actually see how much K-State had to offer.

> **If I had spare football tickets and put two on my windshield wipers, I would come back and find four more with them.**

When we grumbled about not having a winning team, it was more of a pride thing that we wanted to have something we could brag about as opposed to them going: "Our team is better than your team, na na na-na na."

Being a K-Stater in Lawrence is fun. It's frustrating. It's exciting. It makes you feel like a rebel. Every time KU beats us in something, they can say: "Look at that, we beat you again." I can look at them and say I went to a quality university and got a quality education. That's what I went there for.

Moving my son, Jackson, to Lawrence was the hardest thing we ever did. But he has been an avid K-State supporter. He is a scrappy little wildcat.

JOHN FIORE
Lawrence, Kansas

Fiore moved to Topeka, Kansas, immediately following KU's 1988 NCAA basketball championship. But he liked K-State and became a K-Stater in 1993. He almost turned down a job just because it was in Lawrence. Fortunately, he took it, and met the KU grad he would eventually marry.

We had a house-divided tag, but now we have his and her cars. She's got a blue car with KU stuff on it. I have a purple car with a K-State license plate.

I moved from Texas to Topeka when I was about 13 years old. KU had just won the National Championship game, and all signs pointed to me being a KU fan. I don't know if it's a predisposition for always cheering for the underdog or that I just liked the color purple better.

A couple of years later my sister, Tina, ended up going to K-State because some of her friends went there. I went up to visit her in the cool college town and immediately fell in love with the campus and Aggieville and the community. After that first visit I knew that was where I was headed, too.

I had been to Lawrence with the family, and I just didn't feel like it was anything special. It didn't impress me as much as Manhattan, except for Buffalo Bob's Barbecue. It didn't grab me like Manhattan did. I just remember coming back from Manhattan thinking: "Boy, that's the place."

My decision had already been made, but watching the Copper Bowl with my family, and my sister and her friends, really solidified it. I am a lot bigger football fan than basketball fan. Being a big football fan, that made me realize I was going to the right place.

I am more of a basketball fan now. But I think I almost got burned out on being a basketball fan at an early age because of living in Topeka and everybody being so ga-ga about KU basketball. I didn't want to hear about it.

And really, why would I like basketball? That was a KU thing. I had no clue of the K-State history. Now that I've heard all about Mike Evans, Mitch Richmond, Rolando Blackman, Tex Winter and the Triangle offense coming right out of Manhattan, Kansas, it's a lot more relevant to me now.

I graduated in December of 1997 with a degree in criminology. I made it to the final cut when I applied to the Highway Patrol, but I didn't get the job. So here I was, a college graduate, making $6 an hour working as a graveyard shift security guard in Manhattan. I was looking for a job and asked my company if they had anything else.

They said: "We have the security position at Lawrence Memorial Hospital."

I said: "What else do you have?"

They said: "It pays $9 an hour."

I said: "How soon do you want me there?"

That was a Thursday, I interviewed on Friday, and started to work there on Monday.

I didn't get to see many K-State games for a few years because I was working 60-70 hours a week and on Saturdays. And it was a shocker when I got the first mailing from the Alumni Association about football tickets. It was like $320 for a season ticket. I thought: "Holy crap, they were $60 last year when I was a student, and for another $20 you could sit at the 50-yard line."

Now they want way more and are going to sit me up in the corner. So, as much as I would have liked to have kept the season tickets, I couldn't. But by that time they were successful and most of the games were on TV, anyway.

After working at the hospital and getting to know people, I really started seeing Lawrence was a pretty nice community – though I wouldn't admit it at the time. But it was good enough to not be too repulsed by the idea of living here.

I met my girlfriend while I was working at the hospital. The girlfriend becomes my wife, and the ties to Lawrence just get that much stronger. She goes on and does her Master's at KU.

But I still wasn't seeing many games, and I was complaining to a buddy named Kevin Lashley about how I never get to watch the games or go back to Manhattan. He told me about this group called the Catbackers and that they get together on Tuesday nights at a place called Conroy's Pub to watch a replay of the game.

I said: "You're kidding me. They do this in Lawrence?"

They cut out all the commercials and it takes like an hour-and-a-half. You have a few beers and you're with a group of K-State fans. I said: "Hey, that sounds like my kind of group."

So I showed up at Conroy's the next Tuesday, alone. I walked in the door wearing purple, not knowing what I was going to find. You walk in the door wearing purple, the bartender looks at you and points to the door to the side room. They knew I didn't belong there. But I walked in the side room, and there were about 15-20 people all sitting there in front of the big-screen TV.

They saw I was wearing purple and welcomed me as a friend. I sat down there next to a scraggly, long-haired guy, and he said: "Hey, John, how are you doing?" I knew I was among my people and my friends.

That's what K-State is all about. They are good, honest, down-to-earth people. Like I said, I walked into this room of people I had never even met, but I wasn't worried because I knew they were K-State fans and so was I and I would be welcomed. It was absolutely true.

They didn't turn up their nose at me. I was a young kid, and they could have thought, well, this kid doesn't have money so we don't want him in the club. It was not about that. It was like, come be a part of the family.

My wife sometimes comes to the things, begrudgingly. She came and helped us set up for the auction when I was president. I was so proud she was going to be there and help us because she knew how important it was to me and she could see how good a group of people it is. And she shows up wearing a blue-and-red shirt.

Being a Lawrence Catbacker, you have to be tolerant. You have to live amongst them. I have talked to Catbackers who live in Kansas City and Topeka, and they hate Jayhawks. There isn't a good Jayhawk out there.

You can't be like that if you live in Lawrence. Lawrence is a good place to live. It has a good economy . . . and culture . . . and other than all these Jayhawks, it isn't bad.

GORDON LONGABACH
Lawrence, Kansas

Gordon is a Pittsburg State grad who came to K-State later in life when he was a major in the Army stationed at Fort Riley. He was at the original meeting for the Lawrence Catbackers in 1989.

I lived on Vaughn, about three blocks west of the stadium when I was finishing my Master's at Kansas State. Those were the good old days when you could just walk down and buy a ticket and watch Lynn Dickey.

I remember the first time I saw Purple Pride there. I had never heard of it, and there was this lady who had on a purple blouse, a purple jacket, had a purple purse – all different shades – and purple lipstick. For all I know, it may have been Vince Gibson's wife.

When I lived in Manhattan, I went to the old Ahearn and saw KU play there, and everybody would stomp on the stands. Usually they would beat KU. Jack Hartman was the coach then. Those were some good times. But I sort of lost track after I left the area. I was in the Army, going back to Viet Nam and going to Germany for three years. You really couldn't follow them.

It wasn't until 1993 that I really started buying purple clothes and things and started getting hooked on the bowl games. Of course I was at the game when we first beat KU over here in Lawrence. We tore the goalposts down and everyone thought that was crude and rude. Of course Snyder sent Bob Frederick (KU athletic director) $2,500 for the goal post. I think at that time that was how much it cost.

And I never will forget the first time over here when KU beat K-State after all those years when we won. Down come the goalposts. Of course it wasn't so crude or rude when they were doing it. One went up and was thrown into Potter's Pond, and the other went downtown and ended up being thrown over the bridge into the Kansas River. It was a different story then, I guess.

I remember when Al Bohl became the athletic director at KU. The first thing he said was "I got to get rid of all these damn Powercat license plates here in Lawrence." That was in Snyder's glory years, and everybody wanted a Powercat on their car.

But right now, I think they have to prove themselves again. That's my way of thinking about it. And I think a lot of people are that way. The jury's out in both basketball and football. Right now it's kind of a sad thing.

> **" I was somewhere up on the KU campus and stopped at a stop sign. This girl saw my Powercat on the front, and she went over and pretended like she was throwing up on my car. She didn't, but she was a good actress. "**

I'll have to tell you, right now I am down. I don't like seeing KU win three years in a row, and I'm afraid they have the upper hand this year. I guess I am a pessimist, but really, I think I am a realist.

They've got their work cut out for them. They have to rebuild things, in my opinion, and I don't think it's just going to be automatic. A lot of people, last year, were leaving the football games before they were over. These were games where you were getting beat, and they were just looking pathetic, so it's going to be interesting to see what happens.

But I know I am not going to KU's games.

Here's a story. Not long ago, I was somewhere up on the KU campus and stopped at a stop sign. This girl saw my Powercat on the front, and she went over and pretended like she was throwing up on my car. She didn't, but she was a good actress.

DICK LUMEN
Overland Park, Kansas

Lumen works in Lawrence and says it's kind of fun to have a Catbacker club in Lawrence that raises money to support scholarships for Douglas County seniors who decide to attend Kansas State.

Neither my wife, Mary, nor I are graduates of K-State, but a bunch of my wife's family was. My two nephews (Dirk and Travis Ochs) played football at Kansas State. We had followed them through their high school careers, and when Dirk decided to go to K-State we just kept right on following. He started at K-State right after some guy name Bill Snyder arrived.

Nobody knew at the time what would happen. Dirk and Travis' mom and dad, another aunt that lives in Lawrence, an uncle who lives out west, and two or three friends became like family to us. We became a real close-knit group, and it became such a family-and-friend event that we never gave a second thought to not being a part of it. It was just a given that we were going to go wherever the games were.

We don't go to as many out of town games as we used to, but we still go to all the home games. We meet our friends up in the parking lot at the stadium, before and afterwards. They are just really good, salt-of-the-earth type people who really love being around each other. I think that's what kept us going back and going back and going back to all the K-State events.

When Mary and I moved back to Kansas City from Texas in 1987, we became season ticket holders at Chiefs games and the Royals games. When Dirk started playing at K-State in 1992, we were still going to the Chiefs games, and we were going to the K-State games to watch Dirk.

Some weekends when both were playing at home, Monday mornings were a little difficult. We would go to the K-State game, stay in Manhattan and party all night with our friends. Then we would get up, go to the Chiefs game and drag back to our home in Overland Park about 6-7 of an evening and just collapse.

It became obvious that something had to go, and it was a very easy decision. We had acquired a new family. The Chiefs games were far from that. When we looked by comparison, the fans at the K-State games were our friends. Even if we didn't know somebody, we knew them. It was easy giving those Chiefs tickets up.

A couple of things pulled me to the Lawrence Catbackers. Mary's brother, Jake Ochs, lived in Lawrence, and we spent a lot of time with them playing golf over at Alvamar. I had gotten to know a lot of people in Lawrence, so it seemed natural.

And of course it's kind of fun to have a Catbacker group in Lawrence.

I guess my defining moment as a Catbacker in Lawrence came when I was addressing a group of alumni out at the fairgrounds three or four years ago. The alumni, I am told, had always kind of looked down on the athletic supporters, thinking all we did was support athletics.

But I can remember standing up there, and I told them that the previous year we had sent $10,000 to Kansas State – money we had raised at the golf tournament and a little football kickoff thing and some other donations. I remember thinking how cool it was to be able to say we had pulled $10,000 out of Lawrence and sent it to Manhattan for kids.

We support a couple of scholarships for graduating Douglas County seniors who are going to K-State. Not athletic scholarships, just kids going to K-State. I could see the eyes of the people out there in the alumni audience thinking: "Whoa, these are the athletic guys, the guys who get together and drink beer and watch football games and basketball games. They did what?"

It was really cool and kind of defined what we did as Lawrence Catbackers, that we went out and raised money and we did it for kids.

I think the Lawrence group is a little different from some others because of where we are. Even though the people are very involved and get wrapped up in the competitiveness between the schools, in the end we K-Staters tend to find the fun in the event more than some people at other schools. We just can't seem to get too wrapped up in all the seriousness.

I know from my friends, the people we hang out with, sure we are always looking to win every game. That's the nature of people. But if we don't, we do it the right way and all of us have fun together. How much more can you really get out of those things?

Fans of some schools are just unbelievable how hard they are on the players and the coaches. If they lose, you know how disappointed they are and how hard they prepared themselves and how hard they worked. They really want to win those games, and they play their hearts out. There has been a pretty dark period here recently, and I am glad it is over with. The fans were getting a little restless.

Many of us hope that Coach Snyder hasn't taken on more than he can handle. It's just amazing to me that he has taken on this job. It is a total lose situation for him. He doesn't have that much to gain. If he brings it back, it's sort of like "Well, it's Coach

Can you read this?

Mizzou Tigers can't.

Snyder, of course he brought the program back." But if he doesn't I'm afraid people are going to look at him and say all those years were just flukes because look at him now.

LEON ROBERTS
Olathe, Kansas

Roberts' family moved to Lawrence when he was in high school, and as a senior in 1988 he was celebrating with the rest of Lawrence after the Jayhawks' NCAA basketball championship. But after one trip to Manhattan, he eschewed any thoughts of becoming a Jayhawk himself.

I was looking around for colleges, but when I visited K-State everything turned around for me. My dad went to the University of Nebraska, and my grandparents still live in Lincoln. That was my team. My dad is a national bank examiner, and we moved around quite a bit. I grew up in Colorado. My dad was transferred to Kansas City, but my parents like the town of Lawrence.

But I still rooted for Nebraska. There was never an attachment other than Nebraska until I made that trip to Manhattan.

My mother and I were there with other prospective students and their parents. They do a little intro and then walk you around the campus. One of the most impressive things is that when we were walking around with our parents, there were students at Kansas State waving hello and saying we should come to K-State.

This is not a knock against KU, but it never happened that way at KU – even when I was not there with my parents. There was a different feel at Kansas State. Everyone was so friendly. But it gets even better.

After we were done with the tour, the groups are split up and my mom and I are just walking around Anderson Hall. This gentleman in a suit walks up and introduces himself. He asked if we enjoyed our time, and of course we did. He introduced himself as Pat Bosco (dean of students at the time). He asked for our name, and we had a little short chat and he was gone.

Two days later I get a handwritten note from him in the mail: "Nice to meet you the other day. I hope you had a nice time and hope to see you this fall at K-State." That right there sold me 100 percent, and I have been forever a K-State fan.

I have a sister and brother who grew up in Lawrence and who ended up going to K-State, as well. My brother was iffy about K-State. I called Pat Bosco and told him about my story and asked if he would do the same with my brother. He did, and my brother ended up going there, too.

I don't think any of us hated KU when we were growing up. I don't think any of us even thought about it. But once we got to K-State things changed. We had a pretty good view of what KU was all about from living in Lawrence. When we get together, we don't like KU. And to be honest, I couldn't care less what they think of us.

Of course I had tickets to the games when I was in school. I have had season tickets since the fall of 1993 when I got out until now. When we beat Nebraska in 1998, even as a 28-year-old, I may have cried. I don't remember for sure, but I was probably pretty close to it. That was a pretty exciting moment for us.

I did not go down on the field. I sat there and probably waited until every person left. I am 16 rows up, in that end zone where they ripped that goalpost up. I sat there and watched them, then I met them down in Aggieville. It was great.

I was also in St. Louis, and there is a story to this, too. Matt Davis, a friend, and I were staying in a hotel that is attached to the Edward R. Jones Dome.

> **"** When we beat Nebraska in 1998, even as a 28-year-old, I may have cried. **"**

We walked to the game, and all of a sudden Miami beats UCLA which opens the door for us to go play in the national title game. We were up 18, I think. Matt got on the phone and booked us tickets for the National Championship game that we were never able to use.

And even though we were staying at that hotel right across the street, we drove to the outskirts of St. Louis to eat dinner after the game – 30 minutes and 30 minutes back because we didn't want to be around anyone. That was a very quiet four-hour ride home, too. We were both – and probably all of the K-State nation – depressed for at least a month.

As a young adult, if a football game can teach you a life lesson, I guess that one did. There are a lot more important things than a football game. To be that depressed that long over a football game is pretty silly. That was devastating, though, to be up like we were that late in the game and to know we were going to the National Championship game with that team against Tee Martin's Tennessee squad.

My best fan moment is probably the championship game in 2003, but I still think it's my fault that the program has fallen on hard times since. I went to the bathroom at half-time and sold my soul to the devil if we could just win that game. I said that's all I want. So I think it's kind of my fault.

Here's an oops for you. I had basketball tickets in the three years before I bought my business. And when we were

> **"I went to the bathroom at halftime and sold my soul to the devil if we could just win that game."**

really terrible in basketball they had the six-packs that you could buy a package of six games for $99 and we would drive up for the games.

But Wooldridge's last year when we won in Lawrence, another friend and I go up to the game. My parents, who still live in Lawrence, bought me tickets for my birthday. We go to the game, and we're so upset with the way Wooldridge is coaching – armchair quarterbacking this whole deal. We are down by double digits, so we decide we're going to leave at halftime. We leave, and K-State comes back and wins. I was really embarrassed to have to admit that.

TAYLOR HOYT
Ames, Iowa

Hoyt took a different path than his high school classmates at Blue Valley North, many of whom were KU fans. He opted to be a K-State fan, and even as a student at Iowa State, he wears the purple.

I didn't have a single family member I can recall who went to K-State. My parents went to St. Olaf's College. My sister went to Butler University in Indianapolis. I guess one of my mom's cousins went to K-State, but I don't really have any connection to her as far as influencing me.

Everybody I went to school with was pretty much a KU fan, and I was one of those people who didn't want to be a fan of the same team as everyone else. So I became a K-State fan about the mid-1990s or so. That's when I was in seventh or eighth grade and started to get into football. I started watching K-State football and have been a fan since 1998 or 1999 when I started watching them.

Taylor Hoyt (K-State jersey) is outnumbered in this photo of his Iowa State friends (from left) Kyle Debner, Drew Jacobson, Cy Fox and Bill Maurer.
Photo courtesy of Taylor Hoyt

I really enjoyed watching the players and then following them through the NFL. Terence Newman and Darren Sproles and players like that, who succeed in the NFL. I didn't get into their basketball team as much until more recently.

I was looking at K-State and Iowa State, and when I visited K-State I didn't necessarily get the best vibe from the campus. The sports program was almost enough to just make me go there. I came here (Ames). I really liked the campus. The hotel, restaurant and institutional management program was ranked better at the time than it was there. I found a fraternity up here, and I enjoyed the guys who were here.

I'm not involved with the fraternity any more, and I almost transferred down to K-State at the beginning of last school year. But I never pulled the trigger to get the transfer, and after that there was no point to do it because you can only transfer 65 credit hours and I would have had to go to school for a fifth year. I didn't see that being very necessary.

I went to my first K-State football game in person last year (2008) when Iowa State played down there. That was just an awesome game (a 38-30 K-State win). I got free tickets from the manager of the Iowa State football team, and I was sitting with all the Iowa State players' parents and donors. I was sitting there with K-State clothes on in this big island of Iowa State fans.

I really wanted K-State to win, but as far as both teams making good plays I really couldn't go wrong because I was going to school at one place and grew up watching the other one. The Iowa State fans said a couple of things at the start of the game, but when the game starts, they don't say anything. They haven't really had a good football program in quite a few years.

I had only been to Bill Snyder Family Stadium one time before, and there was no game going on. Since my parents weren't fans, I didn't really get a chance to see K-State games when I was younger. My friends and I ended up walking around the parking lot before the game. They told me this was a small tailgating game because Iowa State wasn't that big of a draw.

I have had (Iowa State) season passes for football and basketball since I have been here. I have been to the K-State basketball games here. There are very few K-State fans up here, but I wouldn't say it's hard to be a K-State fan by any means. When I went to the Iowa State-K-State basketball game when (Michael) Beasley came up here, I saw a couple of Beasley jerseys when I was at the game.

I couldn't tell if they were from the area or if they were K-State fans following the team. Ames is the kind of community that everybody likes Iowa State, but most of them have a No. 1 team they like. In some cases that is the Iowa Hawkeyes, which I don't understand. But one of my roommates is a Wisconsin Badger fan. He worships Wisconsin football. I sit there and watch him die as they fall apart down the stretch. Lately, I have been kind of disappointed down the stretch, too, but K-State has been doing better than Iowa State.

It's sometimes hard to follow K-State because we don't get them on television up here as often. We have the Big Ten network up here. So sometimes I see them on ESPN, and sometimes you get flashes when I am watching other games. But I follow them on Gamecast, and ESPN is set up to text me with scores. But as far as live video, I haven't been able to see them as much unless I am at home.

CHAPTER 5
Fans from Afar

While the majority of Kansas State students are from the state of Kansas, there are a few who come from out of state – way out of state – like Buster Renshaw, who came from Anchorage, Alaska, to study at K-State. After graduation they may head home for careers.

But they like to keep track of their Wildcats.

So do K-State grads who scatter to different corners of the world, whether it be Dallas, Orlando, Washington D.C., or New York.

The Kansas State Alumni Association has "Spirit Clubs" or watch parties in 37 states and the District of Columbia. They range in size from a handful of members to the thousands.

The Internet has clearly made it easier for relocated Wildcats to keep track of their teams. And the expansion of sports cable TV networks has made it even easier to catch the Wildcats while sipping an adult beverage or two with their friends who are wearing purple.

But that doesn't mean the passion for Kansas State sports is any less fervent.

✹ ✹ ✹

JILL VINDUSKA
Orlando, Florida

Vinduska sports a Powercat smack dab in the middle of the orange on her Florida license plate, and owns at least 15 pieces of purple clothing. Upon moving to Orlando, she found the K-State Spirit Club looking for a new leader. She now has a mailing list of more than 200 Wildcat fans in central Florida. They hang out at Friday's Front Row on International Boulevard. She has even converted some co-workers into K-State watchers.

I grew up watching K-State sports with my dad, lying on the living room floor. Back then it was only basketball that was really on TV. The first football game I went to was the first time we had beaten Nebraska at home (1998) after years and years and years.

Jill Vinduska organizes the K-State watch parties in Orlando, Fla.

Photo courtesy of Jill Vinduska of Orlando, Fla.

My sister was in college, so I got to experience the mayhem that was K-State football right there. I was sold after that.

Both of my parents went to K-State. My dad's brother did, and one of my older sisters. I had a choice of going somewhere else, but I didn't want to. I had visited KU and other campuses. But I visited K-State my senior year in high school, and I was just amazed. The feeling was completely different. It was just like coming home.

That was so comforting for somebody moving from a small town (Pilsen, Kansas).

My parents were there in the 1960s. They went to just about every basketball game and loved watching it. When my older sister was there in the 1990s was when football was on the rise. So we have hit just about every milestone.

I moved to Florida to try something different, and I ended up staying in Orlando for the last couple of years. I was looking for a club locally, and when I contacted the Alumni Association they said the leader of the club down here had moved away. So I decided to take it over.

We will have anywhere from 10 to 15 people who are there for every single game. For the bigger games, like KU, we will have upwards of 50. It's amazing.

The bar where we watch games together is in the main tourist area of Orlando, so we will have people just walk in when they see the Powercat on the billboard outside. They will just come in to watch games if they are on vacation or traveling. It's crazy.

I have met people I actually knew in college. We hung out in the same social circles or we had classes together, or somehow we were connected.

I do have a co-worker who watches games with me every now and then, which is funny. And I made my boss – we were traveling on business in Kentucky – and I made her watch the KU game with me last year. She is so *not* into basketball, but she sat there and laughed at me the whole time when I yelled at the TV.

I have a Powercat necklace that I wear all the time. I'm actually known for it at work, and they usually use some reference to Kansas when we talk. They will call me Wildcat, and they know every Friday during the football season I am wearing purple in preparation for the next game.

To me, being a K-State fan means it's family. There is nothing like seeing somebody in a K-State shirt and knowing that you immediately have this common bond. You can go and talk to them, and everybody shares their experiences. There is this huge sense of family.

A big part of that, of course, is with my immediate family. But the whole community of K-State is like that, and you run into K-State people all the time. People honk at you on the road if they see a Powercat license plate now and then.

> **❝ I think our alumni group here probably drinks a little more beer when we lose. ❞**

It is such a community. It's amazing, and it just pulls you in.

I support them no matter what, but we do have such a good history with athletics. I have high expectations with Coach Snyder coming back this football season. The first thing I told my parents is that I want bowl tickets for Christmas. That's my expectation.

He has a hole to dig himself out of, and you know things aren't going to get better overnight. But there are always reasonable expectations. But I will watch every game that is on TV, no matter what, win or lose. I think our alumni group here probably drinks a little more beer when we lose.

I always make it back for at least one football game. This season I'm coming to the Iowa State game in Kansas City.

BEN FENWICK
Arlington, Virginia

Fenwick grew up in the shadow of KSU Stadium but actually applied to attend the University of Kansas. An admissions snafu in Lawrence saved him. Now he hangs out in the nation's capital and helps organize watch parties for the K-State faithful.

I had that classic moment – I wanted to get out from where my parents lived and be somewhere else. But KU said I had forgotten to send them something I had sent them. A couple of weeks later they voided my application. After that came, it was "OK, I'll just go to K-State." It turned out to be a very good decision.

My family moved to Manhattan when I was three years old. Both my parents had gone to Kansas State and my dad was a professor there. So I had been pretty much a K-State fan since I was a little kid.

We went and watched games when my dad was able to get some tickets. But it wasn't until I got to Kansas State (2001-05) that I regularly started attending. But it was one of the better things during the early 1990s when I first started to realize: "Hey, we have a college football team here." My parents' house was within earshot of the stadium. On game day you could hear the loudspeakers making the announcements and the fans cheering.

Ben Fenwick wearing his purple power tie in front of the nation's capitol.
Photo courtesy of Ben Fenwick

I didn't go to the basketball games when I was there. And I was already gone and missed out on the turnaround with (Bob) Huggins and now with Frank Martin. When I was there it was almost like we didn't have a basketball team. The women's basketball team was something to cheer for.

When I got to Washington, I thought there had to be a D.C. club here. I found out the previous president of the club was one of my friends at Kansas State, Christine Baker. We had been in clubs and organizations together. So I gave her a call and asked where the watch parties were.

I went to the fall dinner, really just to see if I would recognize anyone there. I got to meet some of the much older

K-State alumni members from the 1940s and 1930s, who are in their 70s and 80s now.

That's been one of the most fun things. It was an interesting time conversing with them. The D.C. area has a very large alumni base. I think it numbers in the thousands.

It's a really good mixture of recent graduates who have come to work on the Hill. Some of them are people I knew or knew of when I was going to Kansas State. And others have been here 30 or 40 years and really know the ins and outs. Getting to know them kind of goes back to what I liked about Kansas State and how friendly everyone was and how it's definitely a community-type atmosphere.

There's definitely a change between basketball being the dominant sport in their generation to football being the dominant sport in my generation. There is a definite pride in the sports aspect of things, from their remembering the Ahearn days and the Elite Eight appearances and Blackman and those guys compared to our memories of Michael Bishop and Darren Sproles.

From my generation there is a lot more academic pride, as well. Former President Wefald talked about all the Truman and Goldwater scholars and things like that. For me that was kind of a badge of honor in going to the school. That's also from my parents' perspective in how the university was in the 1980s compared to when I started my freshman year and how much better its reputation had become in a 10-12-year timeframe.

I keep up just reading the newspapers online. I check out the *Manhattan Mercury* and definitely read the *Collegian* a couple of times a week. And friends and family definitely keep me connected to what's going on back there.

BRUCE McMANIS
Thibodaux, Louisiana

Kansas State was never on McManis' radar screen until his father got a job teaching at the university in the 1960s. He now lives in southern Louisiana where he teaches at Nicholls State University. He follows all Wildcats sports and is happy for the Internet and Fox Sports Southwest, where he gets to see a few more of the games.

I was slated to go to school wherever my father ended up taking a job, so it was kind of a freak thing I ended up at K-State to begin with. But I had a great time while I was there.

Basketball was the dominant sport at the time, but actually it was some of the better football that they had in the pre-Snyder era. That was when Vince Gibson was there, and they almost got to .500.

But still, the outstanding joke on campus relative to football was that when we played KU it was the Toilet Bowl because that was the only bowl that either team would get invited to. I was there for that win over Oklahoma, but I was also there for some of those something-to-nothing Nebraska and Oklahoma games.

I moved to Louisiana right after I graduated, and for a while I didn't pay a whole lot of attention to K-State sports. There wasn't much to keep track of, and it was pre-Internet days.

Bruce McManis (left) leads a group of K-State fans in Southern Louisiana.
Photo courtesy of Bruce McManis

So you really couldn't keep up other than on the Saturday afternoon scoreboard show when they put up how bad K-State lost. They didn't spend any time on it unless it was Nebraska and Oklahoma doing it.

So I kind of fell by the wayside for a couple of years. Then as Snyder came in, it started coming around. The media started expanding coverage, and my interest picked back up.

Another K-State grad, Chris Cox, was teaching at Nicholls for seven or eight years. I teach finance, and he taught marketing. With the expansion of the sports channels, some games started getting televised down in our area. We would get together, recruit a couple of friends who liked to drink beer, and bring them with us. It didn't matter whether they were interested in the game or not.

It grew from that, and we finally decided to register with K-State as a watch party. There are about 200 K-State grads down here, which surprised me. But we're spread out quite a bit.

We get a few people showing up in bars to watch games, and we have converted a few local folks to watch with us. But people who would drive two hours to see a game live, are not necessarily going to drive two hours to see it on TV.

When Huggins came in and basketball started getting exciting again, we started doing a little more with basketball. And I get to see the women's basketball team quite a bit when they play the Texas teams. Television still hasn't caught up with college baseball, so I don't get to see much of that.

I haven't really been back to Manhattan since I moved down here, and the only game I have seen live in 30 years was the Texas Bowl over in Houston. It is just a five-hour drive. I am looking forward to catch the ULL (University of Louisiana-Lafayette) game this year (2009). That's about six hours from here.

We have a lot of guys on the staff here at Nicholls who are graduates from Mississippi, Mississippi State, LSU, Clemson ... we get some pretty lively discussions going on, particularly whether the Big 12 or SEC is the better conference.

One thing I find different here in the middle of LSU country is that a lot of the LSU fans have never even been to the campus other than a game. We have more LSU fans on the Nicholls campus than Nicholls fans. The only connection they have is that they live in Louisiana.

That's really different from K-State. Just about any time you talk to a K-State fan, they have some kind of connection to K-State. They have either graduated from there or were a student there for some period of time. They have a real good connection.

You bump into people, and even though there may be a 20-30 year difference in when you went to K-State, it only seems like you were a year apart rather than 20 years apart. Everybody has their favorite dive in Aggieville.

The primary buildings they were in while at K-State, those buildings still look an awful lot like they did. There are a lot of renovations and modernizations, but they look the same.

Right now I keep up with baseball and women's basketball – which we actually are able to catch some of their games on Fox Southwest. I don't get a chance to see volleyball, but I do keep up with it a bit, too.

My expectations of the teams are that they win and stay off the police blotters. A lot of schools have a lot of problems with that. K-State has been relatively free of that, and I am proud of all the coaches who have put character as one of the things they are looking for in addition to strong athletic skills.

BUSTER RENSHAW
Anchorage, Alaska

Renshaw is what he refers to as an Alas-KAN. He's one of the mainstays who watches games with friends in Anchorage, Alaska, at a place called The Peanut Farm. He came to Kansas State because it was economical. But his wife, Chloé, bought him a K-State branding iron so he can put the Powercat on his steaks, and he once drove a 1966 Buick Wildcat given to him by his grandmother ... perfect.

Being here in Alaska, most people only knew of one team in Kansas and that was the Jayhawks, especially after they won the National Championship in 1988 with Danny

Manning. So when I told people I was going to Kansas State, they said: "Oh, the Jayhawks." I said: "No, the Wildcats."

When they started turning it around in football, people knew the distinction when I came back.

When I was looking for colleges in high school, there was a computer that used to spit out all the information on schools. Kansas State was one of them. I looked up the cost, and it was so inexpensive to go to school there compared to the West Coast schools I was looking at.

The Peanut Farm is where K-Staters watch games in Anchorage, Alaska.
Photo by Anson "Buster" Renshaw

I knew my geography, and I knew it wasn't that flat. I had a neighbor from Kansas, so I knew it wasn't all as flat as a pancake. But I did go into the school blind when I visited the campus.

When I first went there, I thought football was big. I didn't realize how big basketball was with people camping out. I went to some of the basketball games, but not all of them. That was fun, and I even tailgated for some of the basketball games, believe it or not.

But it was the perfect time to go to school there, 1990-95. Back then, we had the worst teams. I have pictures of my first game against Iowa State. The student side was pretty full, but you look around the stadium and there are a few people around the 50. Then it was pretty empty.

The turnaround was a great time to be there. It was WOW, we are beating these guys. I remember when we beat Oklahoma, and the Oklahoma guys were just stunned.

We have a spirit club up here I run that is called the AlasKANS. The games come on early, like 8 a.m., so you are getting breakfast. We probably have five or six regulars at a place called the Peanut Farm. It's a sports bar, and it's great.

Nebraska has a huge following up here, 45 people or so. They probably have the biggest following. Probably next will be Oklahoma, then Texas. It's amazing when you see the alumni from the different schools, especially for a big game like Michigan-Ohio State. But then everybody up here is from somewhere else.

Our biggest problem is that some of the guys up here go hunting, and it's: "Do I watch the game ... " or "it's a nice sunny day, do I go hunting?" So it's hard to get those guys some of the time. And some of the alumni up here, and there are quite a few, were used to K-State being a losing team for so long. So they don't ever come. It's kind of hit or miss.

One of the funnest things was in 1998. We had been going to the Peanut Farm to watch these games. And there were some guys from a suburb of Anchorage called Eagle River. And they were all going to watch the Nebraska game on this guy's big-screen TV. I said I wouldn't come because I was going to be watching at the Peanut Farm because what happens if we win – I want to be there to rub it in the face of all those Nebraska fans.

So it was just me and 44 Nebraska fans – I counted them. Every time there was a touchdown, I would be up and "Yeah!" really loud. I mean you have to get right in their face. Then they would score a touchdown and 44 people were "Waaaaaaaaaah!" And the drinks were flowing, and we all know each other.

This was the year we beat them, and I am doing the Brandi Chastain thing, took my shirt off. I had some friends there laughing their butts off. A couple of Nebraska fans bought me drinks. But there were a few who wouldn't even shake my hand. But it was great just to be there and witness me and the 44. I had been there for all those years when K-State just got pounded.

Renshaw and friends: (L-R) Matt Porreca, Mark Vitamvas, Buster Renshaw, Cory Town, and Sterling Curry.
Photo by Anson "Buster" Renshaw

There is a great picture of the quarterback, the Nebraska quarterback, Eric Crouch. Travis Ochs was just grabbing him. He was running forward, and his helmet was on back-ward. It was just great. They didn't catch that one (facemask penalty).

Another highlight, one of the greatest wins was the 2003 Big 12 championship game against Oklahoma. That was almost as good as the Nebraska win because everyone was hyping, saying Oklahoma was maybe the best college team ever assembled. Darren Sproles, I can't help but root for San Diego, and he just keeps getting better.

I went to the Holiday Bowl in 1999. I get on the plane, Alaska Airlines, and fly down to Seattle and then on to San Diego. When I change planes in Seattle, it's all the other purple. I am the only Wildcat on the plane. It's all Husky fans. Then the captain gets on and says "Go Dogs." It was great to beat them, especially since when I was first at K-State that was one of the very first games and we got hammered, 56-3.

My son is a K-State fan. He's only two and he doesn't know it, but he is. My wife sewed him up some K-State diapers. Now I can say: "You don't know it, but you have been a K-State fan since you were in diapers."

I also was back in Kansas the spring of 2000. I was there to see some friends in Kansas City and we drove up to Manhattan for the day. The gates to the stadium were open, and we walked in and I was just running on the field. It was very cool.

It's always fun to talk K-State. I look forward to the fall and the games starting. Getting my early breakfast and get-ting out of the house. As they get worse in the season, they quit televising their games as much.

KELLEE MILLER
New York City

Kellee runs the K-State watch parties at "Ship of Fools," a sports bar on New York's Upper East Side. She sometimes even invites KU fans to the parties because they crave that Midwest connection.

A lot of the people I hang out with here in New York are people I have met through the watch parties. There are people here who I knew in college. But there are also those who I have met through the group that graduated years before me or years after me and we didn't know each other before meeting at the group. But there is a really good rapport. It is very easy to sit down at the table with any of them and strike up a conversation. You always have that point of commonality.

My boyfriend has a theory that he thinks everyone is connected to Kansas because we can be at some random place and there is somebody who has a connection to Kansas. In New York, you think you are never going to run into those people. But it's a small town sometimes.

I had an internship with the *Wall Street Journal* when I was in college and spent the summer here. Then I spent my fifth year in college in Spain. When I came home, after living in the non-car culture and really loving New York, I was adamant about getting back here. So I started sending out resumes and hoping. I moved here in November of 2002, and my parents were planning to come for Christmas. They said all right, Kellee, you need to find us a place to watch the game. So I immediately started looking into the K-State Spirit Club.

I contacted them, and right after that party the woman who was running it at the time said she was going to move back to Kansas City and was looking for someone to take over the planning for the watch parties. I worked right across the street from the venue, and it seemed like a no-brainer to take on the watch party.

I have been planning them ever since. I think this is going into my seventh football season in New York. As the football team gets good and bad our group gets bigger and smaller. Last year was really a disappointing watch party season with so many disappointed fans. It was hard to draw a crowd.

New York City is so interesting because you draw people from Long Island, New Jersey, from the north, from Westchester County. So you want to find a central location. This bar owner has been really great to us. He always gives us the back room. I think he has always liked our group because we are consistent and there every week. Last year we probably disappointed him with our numbers. On a good day we could have 30 to 40 people. I have had 50. But lately it has been more like 20 and some weekends it was 10.

My parents had gone to K-State, and we were up there almost every weekend. We had this incredible parking spot on the alumni side when there was just a chain-link fence between us and the stands. We would pull right up to the fence, walk in, stand in a small line for a burger and sit down and be like the only one in the row.

I sat through some of the bad years in the 1980s. Then just to watch it evolve as we got better and better when I was in high school. When I got to college (1997) it was just a totally different atmosphere. You could just tell every week-end how excited my father was to come up there and watch the games.

It made them really proud to be a part of that group who weathered the hard years and be among the loyal fans who were still there.

My father is a Bill Snyder look-alike. In fact at the tailgates everyone would call my dad "Coach." I think in bars and restaurants he has sometimes been mistaken for him.

When I was looking at journalism schools, I was looking at KU and MU. But when I went to K-State they just made me feel so at home. You almost want to break the family tradition and go somewhere else. But in the end I was so glad I didn't. My parents were up every weekend for games. My friends all would tailgate at their place in the parking lot.

And when you live so far from home like I do now, it's nice to remember those years and remember how close we were and able to get together so much.

Here in New York, the Big 12 schools try to do lots of things together. They have Big 12 happy hours, they try to have a Big 12 night at the Staten Island Yankees. I think all the Midwest schools and the Texas schools – people still like that camaraderie of the Midwest when you are surrounded by New Yorkers.

One of the guys I have known since I started planning the group isn't even a K-State grad. He went to school here, but he said he grew up watching K-State football with his family. And I have friends here who are KU grads, and I have been known to invite KU fans to our watch parties. They usually show up. It's that Kansas connection.

You see a lot of Longhorn hats here. I want to go up to them and say "Go K-State" to their face or something. I remember one Saturday we were playing Texas, and I was on the way to our watch party. I don't think the Longhorn fan noticed I was wearing purple.

As I got off the bus, I shouted "Go K-State!" He kind of looked up and rolled his eyes.

AUDREY MROSS
Dallas, Texas

Mross sat right behind Rolando Blackman in her Psych 101 course, and her first experience at Ahearn Field House in Manhattan was unforgettable. She organizes watch parties in the Dallas area and just lost one of her best volunteers – when Bill Snyder hired Joe Gordon as an assistant coach.

Being an Air Force brat, I had grown up around jet engines and I had heard loud noises before. But my first basketball game in Ahearn ... it made my hair stand on end. I

This photo were taken on March 6th, 2008 in their backyard in Frisco, Texas. "Since we don't get a lot of snow down here in Texas, we were thrilled to be able to make a snowman and of course we had to decorate it Kansas State style. This was also the first time our new son, Landon, had seen snow so it was a special occasion for us." Amber Ross, 2002 K-State graduate.

Photo courtesy of Dustin and Amber (Robinson) Ross

had never heard a venue that loud. It was pretty impressive. I think Bramlage has caught up, but it's not surprising to me that some people say "gosh, can't we go back and play at least one exhibition game in Ahearn?" There is something about the acoustics in that place.

We all went to the football games, but our story was that we would bring a deck of cards and sit in the stands and play Spades because what was going on on the field wasn't that interesting.

When I got out of college I was in Topeka, but I wasn't going to the games. I wasn't doing anything with the Alumni Association. The focus was more on working and those types of things. I didn't recognize how meaningful some of those relationships and connections would be to me later. My focus was on getting my life as an adult started.

My company moved all of us down here to Dallas. I was absolutely thrilled with the prospect at age 24 of moving from Topeka, Kansas, to Dallas, Texas. That's when it really hit home how meaningful those connections could be. I did move down here with 200 of my co-workers, which made the move a little easier. But right away I hooked up with some former K-Staters I had known in school.

I found out they were actually having watch parties, only we weren't watching anything. They were just happy hours in the early 1980s and K-Staters from all over Dallas and Fort Worth would gather and get to know one another. I think it was probably a few years into the Bill Snyder era before we actually began watching games.

Part of the problem was games down here weren't even televised. Once we got into the Big 12, more of the games were televised. But when we weren't playing well our games weren't on TV. So for the first couple of years there were one or two watch parties per season, and that was all anyone expected. As our fortunes improved and we started being on television more often, there were watch parties every Saturday.

We started off at a little mom-and-pop bar called TNT. It was just a little neighborhood bar in a strip mall. It was great, but we started getting so many people showing up we just outgrew it. We tried a rotating approach of trying several sports bars around town and were never satisfied with that. We finally did a spread sheet so we could determine where all our alums lived and were able to select a location central to most of them.

We picked a Fox and Hound bar and grill up in the northern end of Dallas. It was like magic. Right after we did that the numbers of people coming grew and grew. Of course, it was also dovetailing with the fortunes of the football team doing better. At our peak we had about 500 people coming to the games.

We loved the intensity of having everyone together in one big bar. We didn't want to dilute the experience. But we started getting comments from some alums who lived far away who didn't want to drive after they had been drinking and wanted things closer to where they lived. We found two places that were either owned or managed by K-Staters and thought those would be good options. There was another location in Fort Worth and the latest is in a part of Dallas called Uptown. It has a lot of apartments and shops and is very much favored by the younger set. We miss having them at Fox and Hound, but we understand why they like hanging out in Uptown.

A couple of times we have had fans from the opposing team we are playing show up. They would come and sit in what our folks refer to as "our room." Some people will go over and introduce themselves, but some will get their back up about it. What's funny is that they usually come in on a game their team is supposed to win. I can think of two specifically. They start off the day pretty loud and shooting their mouth off. By the time the game was over, they were pretty quiet.

My favorite game? Oh gosh, it has to be the Big 12 championship, maybe because it was so unexpected. We went into the game just wanting to see a good game. I don't think anyone I know expected a win, much less a win of that margin. But it was like a kid's first Christmas that you were cognizant of times 10. I saw people dancing in the parking lot. We stayed in the parking lot after the game and listened to the post-game commentary with the coach. Then we shut down Westport. And I can remember driving through the McDonald's to get some breakfast and at the same time we were on the cell phone calling to book our tickets to the Fiesta Bowl.

I was in St. Louis in the stands, and now I hate that town. But I'll tell you what, that would all go away if somehow we could get Coach Snyder back to that level before he retires. Wouldn't it be the cherry on the cake if he could get to a National Championship? I don't know if we have it in us, but that would be such a happy ending, and I am a sucker for a happy ending.

I saw him at one of the Alumni Board meetings. He seemed totally refreshed and very focused and very sharp. One of his coaches was one of my best volunteers down here in Dallas. Joe Gordon called me in January. He told me to sit down, then said something to the effect of "What's my dream job?" I said, "Coaching for Coach Snyder, of course." There was a silence, then I just went, "NO." He said, "Yeah." I saw their family up in Manhattan and you could not wipe the smile off his face. When I saw Coach Snyder in June I had to chastise him a little bit because he had taken one of my best volunteers.

CHAPTER 6
Back to the Future

Once again, the athletic landscape at Kansas State underwent a seismic shift. Within two yeas of winning the Big 12 football championship, Bill Snyder had resigned and the football program was in freefall.

Snyder's replacement, Ron Prince, who arrived with such promise, was gone in three seasons. After a botched flirtation with TCU football coach Gary Patterson, Snyder was rehired.

Men's basketball, mired in a decade-long plummet of its own, was reinvigorated by the hiring of controversial coach Bob Huggins in 2006. And when he bolted just one year later, the Wildcats looked to an unproven head coach, Frank Martin.

In the background was an unresolved conflict between school president Jon Wefald and athletic director Tim Weiser that eventually would cost the athletic department millions of dollars.

Weiser resigned in early 2008, leaving the athletic department bereft of an experienced leader and in the hands of Wefald's long-time right-hand man, Bob Krause. Questionable financial decisions followed in the next 12 months.

The hiring of a new university president, Kirk Schulz, and his appointment of John Currie as athletic director seemingly has put the ship back on an even keel. Snyder has re-energized the football program. Martin, to this point, has proven to be a far better coach than anticipated

Those events all played out following the 2003 Big 12 football championship and a second trip to the Fiesta Bowl.

Following two seasons in which the K-State football team won just four league games (two in each year), Snyder announced his retirement just days before the season finale.

Wefald went to an old playbook, choosing another relatively off-the-radar assistant coach to lead the Wildcats: Prince, who had been the offensive coordinator at the University of Virginia. There were hopes that he could duplicate the success of the 1990s. And there were successes, to be sure. Kansas State defeated Texas two years in a row, winning 45-42 at home when the Longhorns were ranked No. 4 in the nation in 2006, and following that up with a 41-21 win in Austin in 2007 when the Longhorns were ranked No. 7 in the country.

Prince's critics make the wry observation: two wins over Texas, three losses to Kansas, three losses to Missouri, case closed.

In Prince's first season, the Wildcats earned a bowl berth, losing to Rutgers 37-10 in the Texas Bowl and finishing with a 7-6 record. He followed that up with a 5-7 season. Despite that overall losing career record, Prince was rewarded by Wefald and Krause with a contract extension that increased the buyout of his contract by $900,000 if he was fired.

After another 5-7 season Prince was fired, triggering the buyout clause. Prince's failure was emblematic of what was happening in the athletic department.

Fans had grown increasingly disgruntled as the season progressed as they watched a team they believed had no direction. Following Prince's firing, the same affliction seemed to have infected the leadership of the athletic department with its botched pursuit of Patterson. After word slipped out that Patterson had provisionally accepted the job, he withdrew his name and Snyder stepped in.

As the football program faltered, the basketball team was being reinvented with a new version of one-and-done – for coaches and players.

Controversial coach Bob Huggins was hired to replace Jim Wooldridge in 2006. He bolted for his alma mater, West Virginia, following a first, successful 23-12 year in 2006-07. K-State posted its first winning record in conference play since the 1989-90 season.

His departure left Kansas State with a dilemma. Michael Beasley, one of the top players in the country, had been recruited. But Huggins' departure put the commitment in question, and K-State made what seemed to many to be an expedient move to elevate assistant Frank Martin to the head spot to save the recruiting class.

Martin had never been a head coach above the high school level, and it was his close ties to AAU teams that helped him win the nod. But it worked. Behind Beasley, Bill Walker, and Jacob Pullen – all freshmen in that recruiting class – the Wildcats reached their first NCAA tournament berth since 1995-96, upsetting Southern California in the first round. The Wildcats also defeated the Kansas Jayhawks in Bramlage Coliseum for the first time in the history of the arena.

Martin's second season was nearly as successful. After weathering an 0-4 start in the conference, K-State won seven of its next eight and finished 9-7 and in fourth place in the conference – the first time the basketball team had earned a first-round bye in the Big 12 Conference tournament since the inception of the league in 1995.

If Martin remains, many believe Kansas State can regain its standing in the upper half of the conference, challenging for a bye in the conference tournament in a league that has perennial powers Texas and Kansas.

Women's sports have rarely been as successful as the Wildcats women's volleyball and basketball teams during this time.

Building on its second-place finish in the 2002-03 season, the women's team won its first Big 12 title the following year with a 14-2 mark. The Wildcats advanced to the second round of the NCAA tournament before falling victim to one of the foibles of the women's NCAA tournament in which fourth-seeded Minnesota was playing on its home court.

The only blot on the K-State record is that despite having the terrific threesome of Nicole Ohlde, Kendra Wecker, and Laurie Koehn, the team advanced past the first weekend of the NCAA tournament only once in four seasons.

But a WNIT tournament title followed the 2005-06 season, and by 2007-08 they were back on top of the conference – once again with home-grown stars in Shalee Lehning (Sublette, Kansas), Ashley Sweat (McPherson, Kansas), and Marlies Gipson (McPherson), leading the way.

The women's volleyball team reached the NCAA tournament four of five seasons.

Track and field also continued its success with NCAA champions Christian Smith (mile in 2006) and Scott Sellers (high jump in 2007 and 2009). Smith also represented the U.S. at the 2008 Olympics.

High jumper Kyle Lancaster also was All-America four times, and just this past season two more Wildcats joined that honor roll. On the women's side there were 14 All-America athletes from 2003-09.

The baseball team is in the midst of an unprecedented run of success. Following the completion of the renovation of Frank Myers Field, the baseball stadium was christened

Tointon Family Stadium in honor of Bob and Betty Tointon, the principal benefactors of the stadium improvements.

Longtime baseball coach Mike Clark became the first K-State coach in any team sport to win 400 games when he accomplished the feat early in the 2002 season. He retired a year later with 435 wins – the most of any coach in school history.

Clark's retirement – and the hiring of former Central Missouri State coach Brad Hill – signaled a new run of success. Clark took the Wildcats to their first-ever Big 12 tournament in 2002. In 2008, Hill took the team back to the Big 12 tournament and reached the tournament's championship game.

The following year, the school once again reached the Big 12 championship game, then celebrated its first-ever appearance in the NCAA baseball tournament. The team finished with a 43-18-1 record – the most wins in school history.

✳ ✳ ✳

GARTH GARDINER
Ashland, Kansas

Gardiner is a staunch K-State basketball fan who routinely makes the 4-1/2-hour drive to and from a Wednesday night game. He grew up on the Gardiner Ranch near Ashland having to position his radio at just the right place on his window sill to tune in Kansas State basketball games, and he still only got about one-third of Dev Nelson's play by play.

I was born in 1967, so my youth was pretty much in the 1970s and 1980s, and growing up as a child I used to dream of playing for Coach (Jack) Hartman. I would listen to as many games as I could out here. Of course, they turn the power way down on those stations at night, and I had to prop the radio up on the window sill at just the right angle to hear.

But growing up having heroes like Rolando (Blackman), Eddie Nealy, Chuckie Williams, Mike Evans, and Curtis Redding, I just became really passionate about K-State basketball. I took some heat for it because I was such an avid fan as a kid growing up. Obviously, when your team doesn't do well, the fans of certain other schools like to jump on you.

As a kid I always wanted one of those autographed basketballs they had at the Catbacker auctions. But they were bringing $300 or $400, and that was more money than I could afford on my measly allowance. I went to Dodge City for a Catbacker event with some local K-State alumni here in Ashland who invited me to ride with them.

I had a pretty substantial scrapbook of clippings, everything from the *Wichita Eagle*, the *Hutchinson News, Sports Illustrated*, whatever I could find. I would always take it up to Coach Hartman to let him look at it and autograph it for me. So he kind of began to remember me from meeting me at all those Catbacker events.

Well, this particular year I took a little rubber basketball that I played with in my parents' driveway up there with the hope I could give it to Coach Hartman and see if he would take it back to Manhattan and get it autographed. He was always very kind, always called me "Podner." He called everybody "Podner," but I didn't know that then. Anyway, he took that basketball back with him.

This was like in April or May sometime. June rolled around. July rolled around. No basketball. No basketball.

The wind was just coming out of my sails. I had told every-body how I had given the basketball to Coach, and he was going to get it signed and get it back to me. They would keep asking if I had gotten the basketball yet, and were all say-ing: "Yeah, Coach Hartman is probably really enjoying your little rubber basketball. They are probably practicing with it up there."

One day in October, I got a box, and it was from K-State. Inside was a brand new leather autographed basketball with all the signatures on it: Rolando Blackman, Ed Nealy. I think it was from Rolando's sophomore or junior year. That just made my day. It was one of the most prized possessions I could have ever had. To this day I still have that ball, and it's in a little acrylic case I had made for it. It's down in the basement. The kids know not to touch that ball.

From that time I developed kind of a unique and special relationship with Coach because he kind of remembered me. I was in junior high, and I wasn't a very good basketball player, but I always dreamed I could play for him. I would go to his camps in the summer and things. He would always come up and shake my hand and ask how things were going. He always remembered my name. In fact I was standing next to what they called the ovens in Ahearn the summer of my senior year in high school. I was standing next to Mark Dobbins when Coach offered him a scholarship. I was kind of thinking he was talking to me, but he wasn't looking at me.

At K-State I lived in a fraternity house right there by Ahearn called Farmhouse Fraternity. Coach would park his car right there in that No. 1 parking spot just north of Ahearn. A lot of times I would see Coach when he was pulling up to work and I would be on my way to class. I would stop and we would visit a little bit, then go on our way.

I remember really well when he announced his retirement. I snuck into the press conference. I was just heartbroken that Coach was retiring, especially the way he went out.

After that we went through the Lon Kruger years with Mitch (Richmond) and Steve (Henson). That fanned the flames again. I was in Manhattan and remember when we beat Purdue to go to the Elite Eight (in 1988), the place was just crazy. Then we play KU to go to the Final Four after we had already beaten them twice that year.

I am still so mad at Scooter Barry (KU guard), I could hit him right in the gut. The guy doesn't score in double figures his whole life and he lights us up. That was a real knock-the-wind-out-of-you deal.

I wasn't very much of a football fan because we were so awful. I graduated from high school in 1985. I got to see them win two or three home games in four years of college. I went to the games; you had to. It was part of your social activity.

The parking lots were gravel. You would walk up and get your chair on the wooden bleachers. Any time five minutes before kickoff you could find a spot. But most of the time there was more action in the bleachers than there was on the field, either with people drinking too much and getting into a fight or passing out.

But I was a K-State fan so I supported the football program by going to the games. It wasn't very much fun.

Then they hired this offensive coordinator from Iowa who was supposed to be the wonder child. I went over to the union when they had the press conference and listened to him talk. I was like: "OK, here we go again."

He's not fire and brimstone. I don't know when I bought my first football season tickets, probably a couple of years after I graduated. Started going back to games and going to the bowl games and things like that.

In basketball, to be honest, I went into a hibernation period when we went through those years after Coach (Dana) Altman left. I was very frustrated and voiced my opinion pretty regularly to the athletic directors.

When they hired "Hugs" (Bob Huggins) I was all in again and still am. The day they hired Hugs I called and ordered five season tickets. I was a college basketball fan, and I liked his teams because they played so hard and he was so intense. I thought if you are going to play the game, you should do it all out.

The thing that I will always cherish him for is revitalizing K-State basketball. It's because of him that we have the basketball program we do. I got to know him and Frank (Martin) and the guys on the staff, and because of my relationship with them I have become even more passionate about the basketball program.

The interesting thing about Frank is that with his background he couldn't be further from being a Kansan. But he is very much like K-State. He's got a blue-collar ethic, kind of a chip on your shoulder. And he is such a loyal person. He'd jump in front of a bus for you if you were part of his family.

I think he appreciates the fact he was given an opportunity by K-State to be a head coach. If he will continue to be given the type of support from the administration and fan base, he could be there for as long as he wants to be. The only thing that bothers him is empty seats. It really bothers him to walk out of that tunnel and see a half-filled coliseum.

That's one of the frustrating things for me because living here it is hard to get back to as many games as I would like to, especially with having kids now. But you hear about the people in Topeka or Kansas City even, and they say: "Well, I'm not going to a Wednesday night game and have to drive an hour over and an hour home to the game." Guys ... I have driven 4-1/2 hours to a Wednesday night game and then driven home.

I don't know what you can do about it other than continue to build the program. Eventually it will be like the old days, doesn't matter what day of the week, or who you are playing, it will be full just like it is in Lawrence. I am really excited about where the basketball program is headed and the people who are running it.

It's harder now to get to as many games as we would like with three kids: two boys and a girl. My oldest son, Greysen, he's starting to drink the Kool-Aid pretty heavily. The other two, Gage and Grace, are still young enough that we are brainwashing them. But they will probably fall in step.

I met my wife, Amanda, in Manhattan. Her parents had gone to K-State. She was involved in collegiate rodeo so she went to Northwestern Oklahoma State University and graduated from there.

My dad graduated from K-State with a degree in animal husbandry as it was called back in the day. He never really was a big sports fan like I kind of turned into being. But he did quite a bit of work with extension beef specialists working on different projects. When he would go up there, I would sneak into Ahearn and try to catch a practice or something.

ALAN AND KATY AMES
Salina, Kansas

Alan is the "K" of the gray-sweatshirted "K-S-U" threesome at women's basketball games. He's been a K-State fan since childhood, but had a hard time following the 'Cats while living in Texas until 2000. Katy is the lady with purple hair in the north end zone at Bill Snyder Family Stadium. She's been a regular at Wildcat football, basketball, volleyball, and women's basketball games most of her adult life. They met on a bus of K-State fans heading to a women's basketball game at Iowa State. She made a lasting impression on him. She loved the way he "Wabashed," and now they're married.

The Ames' wear the KSU sweatshirts at women's hoops games and Katy wears purple hair.

Photo courtesy of Alan and Katy Ames

ALAN: I was divorced in 2000 after 30 years of marriage, and that's when I really became a big K-State fan. I moved back to Kansas from Texas, and I had the opportunity to go to whatever I wanted to go to. I started going to football and women's basketball – not so much men's basketball. But if it was K-State, I was for it.

I found some football tickets through a friend of my dad. So my dad and I, and some cousins (Mike and Althea Wertz) from up in Blue Rapids, Kansas, bought them. We started going to some football games, tailgating and going to the football games in 2000.

Towards the end of the season, I can remember Mike and Althea saying, "have you ever gone to a women's basketball game?" They had season tickets, and they thought the seat next to them was available. It was, so I bought it. We had these gray sweatshirts made up so that we had "K-S-U": mine was a "K" on the front and a "U" on the back. Althea had "S" on the front and back and Mike had "U" on the front and "K" on the back.

I started seeing this lady with purple hair at the games with her daughter. I would see them, but I didn't know who they were. I remember seeing her the first time at a football game. She was standing in the bleachers and the sun was hitting her. I still remember that picture in my mind. I thought she was a player's mom or something. She had a jersey on and purple hair, and who else but a mom would do that.

Then Mike and Althea got a foster child, and they couldn't get away to as many games. It wasn't as much fun going by myself, although I did. I remember going on a bus to watch the women's team play at Iowa State. In the seat right in front of me were a couple of women. We got to talking, and come to find out it was the purple-haired lady. I told her I was the guy in the gray sweatshirt with the big "K" on it. She knew who I was, too.

We became very good friends. We went to all the games together. She is now my wife. So I met my wife through K-State women's basketball games.

KATY: I had seen him. He was always smiling and having such a great time. The whole stadium is kind of a family-fun deal every time the band starts up. Everybody's "Wabashin." He was always a great "Wabasher" and smiling all the time. There is always an attraction to someone who loves it as much as you do.

We have a purple Gold Wing (motorcycle) and trailer that matches and has Powercats all over it. I actually got him to wear purple hair the last homecoming parade. It was called something like Hard Rock KSU. He wore my original hair, and he looked like a Beatle. It got a tremendous response.

Some sorority girls came and got their pictures taken with us. He said he could never get sorority girls to pay attention to him before that.

ALAN: My dad went to K-State and studied mechanical engineering, but he didn't finish. I went to K-State. I didn't finish, either. I never had to study in high school (Long Island, Kansas). When I was at K-State, it was during Viet Nam and probably three-quarters of the guys who were there shouldn't have been. They were there just to stay out of the draft, and it was absolutely impossible to study in the dorm. You couldn't do it, and I didn't know how to, anyway.

I ended up at Pittsburg State and graduated. I ended up one class away from an MBA from Texas-Arlington. But I always told people I had probably learned as much by flunking out of K-State than I did the rest of my college put together.

When I was at K-State for the year-and-a-half, I never missed a basketball game. I had played in high school and had a scholarship to Colby Junior College, but I always wanted to go to K-State.

KATY: I don't know what grade I was in, but the teachers were stalling for time, and she brought us a page into class to color. It was this funny-looking bird with big shoes. As a kid, I thought: "Birds don't wear shoes." One of my classmates said you are supposed to color those yellow. I kind of protested, so they had to look for something else for me to color. I didn't really have a strong family support of K-State. I just kind of went my own direction.

My uncle (Chris Olds) was four years older than me, but he was the closest to my age in the family. He always liked KU, so we would argue. I think because I always liked arguing with him I chose the purple route. Ever since, I have loved K-State. I read everything I can. Even when I was in high school I read everything I could.

But I felt the need to go into nursing, so I didn't go to K-State. But I lived in Manhattan most of my adult life by choice. I just loved it. If there was anything purple going on, I was there.

ALAN: Mike and Althea had always been big K-State fans. They had lived in Phoenix and had gone to all the watch parties down there. They had a Model A with all purple wheels. They moved back, and the timing just worked perfectly where they had the opportunity and were big K-State fans. I was single and had nothing else to do. So we just started going to all the sports.

We got started following the women's basketball, which I absolutely love. It's the kind of game I used to try and play, except they are much better at it than I ever was. I can't really relate to the men's game any more. It's not what we did at all. The women's game is fundamentals and just pure basketball.

The really neat part is that through our following the basketball team, we have gotten to meet all the girls' families. They know us, we know them. It's awesome. I never had any idea it would ever create anything like this. And we follow all the girls in their WNBA careers.

And I love the kind of players that Coach Patterson brings into the program. They are wonderful people, not just good basketball players. Volleyball is the same way. Susie Fritz is an awesome coach, too.

KATY: I was always more of a football fan, but I did everything at K-State. I went to everything I could. Sometimes I would win tickets on the radio, and I was just sort of in tune with everything that was going on because in the early days it was hard with five children to get tickets for everybody.

When I moved back to Manhattan in 1979, I remember buying gasoline and them giving away tickets, saying go out and support the football team. I could take all the children to the game and have them sprawled out all over the benches because there was always room.

I was going to women's basketball when there was hardly anyone there. But it was kind of hit-and-miss until Olga (Firsova) was there. Then we started going all the time. I had season tickets that were G.A. I would have one or two, or sometimes all five children with me, and we would be outside four or five hours before the game just so when the gate opened we could run down and get front-row seats.

It's great because you get to visit with the girls. They just all know me. Now that I am a grandma I sometimes think I need to stop the purple hair because I am an old lady and it is not really cool. But I feel so naked. People say to me every single time: "Where is the purple hair?" Sometimes it is the players who say that.

It's just been so much fun to be part of the transition in football and go through the glory days when it is just so awesome to be associated with K-State. I loved it then, and I love it now. When I hear the band, it just starts all over for me. They used to play the "Eye of the Tiger" in the stadium, and that was just where I wanted to be – no where else in the world but in that stadium and watching those guys warm up. I just really love it. It will be a part of me until I can't make it up the stairs.

ALAN: We didn't go to all the football games last year. My dad was 84, and last year he said he didn't want to. I couldn't quite figure that out, but he's 84 … and we had just moved to a different house and we didn't know how our budget was going to work. So we decided to skip a year. We really, really missed it.

The opportunity arose to go back this year, and I went and talked to dad and asked if he was interested. He said he really missed it. A lot of times there is a volleyball game the same day as the football game, and we used to always take in both. It would make for a really, really long day for him because we would tailgate for the football game and then stay and go for the volleyball game.

But he didn't want to tell us that. When I finally got it out that's what the trouble was, I said we love to have you with us. It's something we do together and very much enjoy it, and it's not the same without you. If that's the problem, we just won't go to the volleyball games. I was so glad to find out what the real problem was because there is a pretty easy solution to that.

KATY: (Former safety) Jon McGraw is the reason for the purple hair. He was a walk-on from Riley (Kansas). I really enjoyed Jon's game when he was a high school player. At the St. Patrick's Day Parade before the first year he played, he was on one of the floats.

I had gone into a store in Aggieville called Déjà Vu, just a funky little store. But up on the top shelf they had this purple wig, and I really liked it. It looked just like hair. I bought it and put it on that day because it was pretty cold and I was using it like a hat. The float came along and Jon saw me and got off and came running up and said: "That's the most awesome hair. If I see that in the stands, I know I have a fan."

I have worn it ever since. I remember being at an Oklahoma game, and I had bought my tickets from an OU fan. I was right in the middle of all these OU students He was in the end zone, and I could tell he was laughing. But he pointed and found me up there.

It cost me $30, but it's been the greatest investment I ever made. I wash it and take care of it. I have six different wigs now, different styles. But it is still my very favorite. I wash it and take care of it like it is a precious jewel because it has brought me so much happiness.

I also have a purple Santa suit. In December, I wear the purple Santa suit, complete with a purple beard. At the Big 12 championship game (2003) I was Purple Santa. Darren Sproles and Ell Roberson knew ahead of time. I got an e-mail from Roberson like a week before the game that said: "Guess what I want for Christmas, Santa?"

GEORGE BREIDENTHAL
Kansas City, Kansas

George fell in love with women's hoops at the 1997 Big 12 championships when he watched Kansas State finish second in the tournament. Now he has tickets to KU men's games and the K-State women's games and his preference is to watch the K-State women.

My father went to engineering school at Kansas State. He didn't graduate, but we would go to the Big 8 Christmas tournament every year. It was a great tournament, and of course we rooted for Kansas State. We went to the Final Four in 1964 when Kansas State was there. That was John Wooden's first championship at UCLA.

So I always followed K-State, even though I don't think they even had women's sports at all.

I started at K-State. But I ended up going to school at Emporia State and graduating and sort of lost track for a while. You are always a K-State fan, but I had gone to Emporia and was a fan of that, too.

I swore I would never go to another men's tournament because I am not a big fan of post-season tournaments. But I think it was probably 1997, somebody gave me a ticket to the women's tournament. K-State did really well; I think they came in second (they did, to Colorado). Andria Jones, Nicky Ramage, Angie Finkes. I thought: "This is a pretty interesting sport."

I kind of like the way the women play below the rim and with better fundamentals. I have seen it change over the years. The women have become stronger, and they are better players because they have started to play at a young age like the boys do. They are playing a better game.

The next year I went to the Ahearn auction and bought a trip with the women's team to one of their games. My son and I have traveled a lot. I thought maybe this would be something my daughter could share with me. We ended up getting to go to two games, one in Des Moines against Drake and the next day at Eastern Michigan.

I really enjoyed it. I didn't have a season ticket because that was in the middle of the year. But I got them the next year, and since then I've gotten to know all the players, the parents, the staff. I am really fortunate. Coach Patterson has taken me to some of the road games.

I have seen some teams with records that are not very good and some that were very good. But the main things I have gotten out of watching the teams is the way she and her staff really seem to care about the players. It is more than I thought college basketball really was. I thought you get some players and you put them out to play. But it is a 24/7 deal.

And I've gotten to know the dedicated parents and families of these young ladies. I know that's not something that very many people get to do. I really appreciate that because you get to know them not only in basketball but outside of basketball. I remember sitting down and talking to Kendra Wecker's dad for an hour in Pennsylvania when Kendra was injured, and talking about what it means to be a father.

Things like that are more important to me than the basketball. I don't really care about the wins and losses. Sure it's more fun to win because the crowd gets excited, and you make it to the tournaments. But as far as a fan, I am going to come to the games, win or lose.

To me the game has become secondary. It's become more of a social thing. It's the game that draws you together, but it's the people who keep you there. I am just lucky to have gotten to know Deb.

The other thing I have found about Kansas State fans is that the ones who are really committed fans never retire and never really go away. If you don't see them at games, you know they have died. If you wear your Powercat hat, somebody comes over and talks to you.

I am sure K-State has some fair-weather fans as well. After Kendra Wecker and them graduated (2005), I was talking to a woman at the Final Four, and she was a K-State person. I asked if they were going to go to the games the next year. She said: "I don't think so. They aren't going to be very good." I was appalled.

FAE AND LAWRENCE ODGERS
Salina, Kansas

The Odgers are the "sign people" at the Kansas State women's basketball games, encouraging the players. Fae laughs, saying she became a K-State fan because "my husband is a bleeding-purple K-Stater." Lawrence says: "Well, that's what she says, anyway."

FAE: We have a company that does videos for weddings, and we had done a wedding several years ago for Amy Short, a girl from out at Goodland, who had been on the basketball team. We got kind of interested. Very shortly after Amy's wedding, we starting coming to the games. We didn't make it except to the weekend games. And we didn't go to out-of-town games except to Colorado because Boulder was closer.

LAWRENCE: We weren't able to actually attend a lot of athletic events until the last 10 years or so. We lived in southwest Kansas and northwest Kansas and it was a long ways to K-State events. When we lived in Atwood it was about 4-1/2 hours from our door to the stadiums. As we would drive past Hays and Salina, we always used to say it sure would be nice to be closer to Manhattan.

Fae and Lawrence Odgers holding signs at a K-State women's basketball game at Connecticut.
Photo courtesy of of Fae and Lawrence Odgers

We would get back for a men's basketball game occasionally, once or twice a year. But for some reason I started listening to the radio and listening to the girls basketball. We finally started going down there more when Nicole (Ohlde) was a sophomore. At the time there weren't many season ticket holders.

One of the neat things, as far as we are concerned, is the opportunity to know the parents and grandparents of the girls on the team. We are on a first-name basis with all the parents. And we do travel some with Ashley's (Sweat) grandparents. They don't drive very well, so we will drive with them several times to out-of-town games.

FAE: We just really enjoy the girls. Shalee Lehning is kind of from my high school territory. I graduated from

Satanta many years ago, so I kind of feel the kinship with Sublette.

Fae and the K-State women's team on Fae's birthday in Fayetteville, Ark.
Courtesy of of Fae and Lawrence Odgers

LAWRENCE: My favorite memories, I suppose, are the ones I had from high school. I grew up in Salina, and my sister and brother-in-law had tickets for the first two or three years in Ahearn Field House. So I would go over there with them back in 1949, 1950, 1951 and 1952 – when they had the good teams with Ernie Barrett and Dick Knostman.

I had never met Ernie Barrett until several years ago. I was checking into a hotel at Garden City, and there was this guy in front of me that I thought sure looked like Ernie Barrett. But he didn't look heavy enough. Sure enough when he got to the desk, he said: "Barrett."

I said you don't happen to be "Ernie Barrett." He said he was, and you know how Ernie is. We just had a real good visit. I was sure glad I finally had a chance to meet the man.

I went to K-State in 1956 after being in the service, and I was in journalism. One semester I was taking photography and got to sit on the end of the court when Jack Parr and Bob Boozer were involved. That was a pretty neat experience. I wish I still had some of those photos. But they were college assignments, and you would turn them in.

How did we become the sign people? I always thought the signs were kind of neat when they were shown on the television and the jumbotron. They have to be catchy and make an impact. We have worked together to find some slogans and phrases. A year or two ago, I can't remember what player it was, one of the parents told their daughter: "I don't know who those people are over there with those signs, but they are a good inspiration to the people coming into the coliseum. That really did make us feel good.

FAE: We're on the front row down close. We have signs for each of the girls and then for anything special coming up. My husband usually comes up with the idea, and then I create the signs.

LAWRENCE: It's been a fun ride. Even when you travel, K-State people find you. A few years ago we were traveling to California. We laid over in Las Vegas. We had our purple on, and sure enough people would come up and talk to you. Not too many K-Staters will walk by you if you have purple on.

JASON BRADLEY
Smithville, Missouri

Bradley didn't attend Kansas State but grew up surrounded by K-Staters who showered him with Wildcat gear every Christmas. The way he figures it, he grew up in Kansas, so what other school could you possibly be a fan of?

It was predetermined I was going to be a K-State fan, and that was it. My grandfather went there, and he would tell me stories of Nichols Gym. He was one of those guys who sat in the rafters. He had these purple cowboy boots he wore around all the time, and a purple cowboy hat. I grew up in Atchison (Kansas), and it should have been KU territory. But we were never KU fans. Never.

My first football game was against New Mexico State (1990). I was in junior high school. It was a night game, real rainy. My dad took me, and we were sitting over in the chairbacks that felt like they were about 12 inches wide. I remember a lady sitting in front of me had an umbrella, and I was getting soaked because it was all running off on me. My first basketball game would have been around the same time. I think it was Delaware State (1991), and we smoked them.

Of all the games I think the USC win (2002) was pretty cool. That was the loudest I ever heard the stadium. When Terence Newman ran that extra point back, that was really cool. That and the Nebraska game in 2000. We had already beaten them once. It was a night game. About halfway through the fourth quarter it started snowing. Willie was on top of the press box doing the K-S-U chant. And with about 10 seconds left we ran out on the field and tore the goal posts down.

We also went to the Big 12 championship game that we lost to Oklahoma (2000). Man it was cold. But the 2003 game was a really special one for our family.

My wife's grandfather, Conrad Feldkamp, passed away a couple of days before the game. We had the funeral that day. We were all the way up in Seneca, Kansas, and there was no way we could get back to the game; and we were going to get slaughtered anyway – so we thought.

We sat there at her grandparents' house with the whole family and watched that game. To see it unfold like it did, after the funeral, that was crazy. That just lifted everybody up that night. And we all thought he had something to do with it in a little way. I'll never forget that night.

Basketball games, I don't really have a favorite because we have sucked for a long time. That KU game a couple of years ago when we beat them, I watched that on TV. I didn't want to go out there because I would get too upset if we lost. So I was watching it on TV. I closed myself in the basement and just watched it. My heart was beating so hard. I couldn't believe we had won that game.

We went to the (KU) game last year, and the atmosphere before the game started was incredible. It was so loud I couldn't believe it. It was a pretty good game for the first 10 minutes, and after that it was awful.

I think it was in Jim Wooldridge's last year, I bought four tickets to the KU-K-State game in Lawrence. My wife graduated from KU – which is a funny story in itself. Her whole family is K-State, and everyone went to K-State except for my wife and her sister. They went to KU. Ridiculous. I don't even know why her dad let that happen.

She still roots for K-State a little bit, but she is a KU fan. And I have another good friend who is a KU fan. He and his wife graduated from KU. So I bought four tickets and thought it would be fun to go out there. I had never seen a game in Allen Fieldhouse.

I kind of scooted away from the three of them, and I was sitting way up in a corner. There weren't many K-State fans there, but I found some. We were down by like 13 points at halftime. Brandon Rush was killing us. Cartier Martin wasn't doing anything. Then that second half turned around. We locked them down, and they couldn't score. Cartier Martin scored like 32 points or something. I couldn't believe we won that game.

Afterwards we went out to eat in Lawrence, and they didn't hardly talk to me the rest of the night they were so mad.

I think the K-State fans are more passionate than fans of some other schools – especially from 1998-2003. We had never been there before, and we just couldn't believe it was finally happening. It was something new for us. I mean we were one fumble away from playing for the National Championship game in 1998. Gol-dang. That was the worst game of my life.

I didn't go to it. I stayed home and watched it with my wife and my parents. I got so mad I threw the remote at the TV. I tore my jersey off and went outside and sat at the dock for a while I was so mad at that game. I was so disgusted that every time K-State football came up for the next month I couldn't even read any stories about K-State football. It was too painful.

That was probably our only shot. That's the way a lot of us feel. We're a small school, not one of the big boys. I think (Mike) Stoops and (Brent) Venable ... those guys already had their minds on Oklahoma and it just let the air out of things. That's another reason it was so sweet when we beat those suckers in 2003.

Photo courtesy of Christopher Hanewinckel

Authors

Kent Pulliam spent more than 30 years as a sports journalist at *The Kansas City Star*, reporting on the Kansas City Chiefs, auto racing, Olympic sports, and Kansas State during the football team's glory years of 1997-2001. He won several writing awards from the Associated Press Sports Editors and the Missouri Press Association. During his time covering Kansas State, the University of Kansas graduate discovered the passion that K-State fans have for their school, the pride they take in the success of their teams – and the ferocious protective feelings they display when they believe their teams aren't getting the respect they deserve.

Rich Wolfe's books have sold well over a million copies in the United States. Wolfe has authored the best-selling books in the history of Notre Dame and the Chicago Cubs. The Iowa native is the only person to appear on both *Jeopardy!* and ESPN's *Two-Minute Drill*. In 2006, he was inducted as one of Leahy's Lads at Notre Dame.